GOOD MORNING!

VOLUME II

A Devotional For Encouragement and Thought

IRVIN F. STAPF JR.

Paperwrights

Paper Wrights, LLC
www.paperwrights.co

CONTENTS

DEDICATION

This book is dedicated to the faithful members of Christ Lutheran Church, TAALC, Germantown, Maryland. Many of you have shared with me and given your support throughout many times of change. You have received God's Word with joy, and grown in the faith and love of Jesus, our Lord and Saviour. You have shown the love of Christ in dedicated service and sacrifice through our various ministries and continue to do so as a Christian fellowship even after my retirement. You have my sincere gratitude and love in Christ Jesus.

The Rev. Irvin F. Stapf, Jr.
September 2024

Our Resolution -
To Grow In Grace

This is the time of year for New Year's greeting, wishing people well for the coming year. I like the way St. John did it with a friend of his named Gaius in his brief letter. [3 John 1:1-2]. "To my dear friend Gaius, whom I love in the truth. Dear friend, I pray that you may enjoy good health and that all may go well with you, even as your soul is getting along well." John desires to see that all goes well with his friend. But more than that, that "his soul is getting along well". Or that his soul "prospers" as in another translation. This becomes the foundation for all the rest of life. There are times when all doesn't go well, or that health fails. What sees us through these times is a soul that has prospered. Soul here in the Greek original is psuche meaning breath. When God created mankind He breathed into them the breath of life and man became a living being. [Genesis 2:7] It is God's breath of life that sustains us in all times, not just the good ones. I have the same desire for each of you - that all would go well with you in this New Year, but even more that through Word and Sacrament, through prayer, study, and the fellowship of believers that you would grow in the grace of our Lord Jesus Christ.

A NEW YEAR

When we embark on the first day of a new year none of us knows what it will hold. There is a well worn yet still true expression that says, "We don't know what the future hold, but we know who holds the future". It will undoubtedly be a mixture of good and not so good as all past years loving-kindness been, but we keep our focus on the One who holds our future. Psalm 59 under scores this as David is praying to God for help against enemies who seek to kill him. After pouring out his need he ends in verse 16 by saying, But as for me, I shall sing of Your strength; Yes, I shall joyfully sing of Your loving-kindness in the morning, For You have been my stronghold And a refuge in the day of my distress." God is our stronghold as another of the Psalms says. He is our strength. And a good practice to begin each day is to declare, "Yes, I shall joyfully sing of Your loving-kindness in the morning." I am certainly not a linguist. I have a enough trouble with English, but I have learned the importance of a few words. The Hebrew word here in the New American Standard Version that it translated "loving-kindness" is the Hebrew word hesed. It is a word that has no full English translation. It is alternately rendered steadfast love or mercy. The loving-kindness of our Lord has a depth that cannot be fully put into words, but it is that lovingkindness into which we are bought as we enter this new year. Whether good or bad happens in these coming days the untranslatable depth of God's loving-kindness will sustain us.

COMPASSION NOT SACRIFICE

Jesus had a number conflicts with the religions leaders of His day, especially over the Sabbath laws. He couldn't break through their religious legalism. Something that hangs on to this day in a number of Christian denominations. They complained about His healing on the Sabbath. He countered with the question of whether it was right to do good or to do evil on the Sabbath. The doing of good superseded strict adherence to the written code. He told them "if you had known what this means, 'I DESIRE COMPASSION, AND NOT A SACRIFICE,' you would not have condemned the innocent." (Matthew 12:7) He was quoting from the Old Testament prophet Hosea which they should have well understood. We have many decisions to make concerning what is right or wrong in various situations. At time we are not 100% sure which is right, but I think Jesus is saying that it is better to err on the side of grace rather than on the law. That doesn't mean that we can ignore God's laws. Our Lord does give us a way of life that is for our best, but we grow into that best by small steps. Sometimes it means that we can let one issue go if it means helping a person grow a little closer to the Lord now. Parents know this well. Our kids are not always where we want them to be, but some battles are not worth fighting just now if we can help them grow little in a more important area. We are God's kids, and we are all seeking to grow more fully in His grace.

WALKING WITH OUR LORD

A great hymn and one of my favorites is Great Is Thy Faithfulness. It was written in the 1920s by Thomas Chisholm as a testament to God's faithfulness through his very ordinary life. One doesn't need to be rescued from life-threatening danger or see God's miraculous provision in the direst of financial crises to truly know the faithfulness of the Lord. God remains faithful day in and day out in the largest and smallest of circumstances. "Chisholm explained toward the end of his life, 'My income has not been large at any time due to impaired health in the earlier years which has followed me on until now. Although I must not fail to record here the unfailing faithfulness of a covenant-keeping God and that He has given me many wonderful displays of His providing care, for which I am filled with astonishing gratefulness.'"* One of the lines in Chisholm's hymn says that we "have strength for today and great hope for tomorrow". Whatever you have planned for this day, whatever tasks you face, the Lord is with you. "The Lord's mercies are new every morning great is Your faithfulness. 'the Lord is my portion,'says my soul, 'Therefore I hope in Him!'" (Lamentations 3:22-24)

*Some information was taken from a Bill Gaither website - gaither.com

SHARE THE VISION

I was thinking about how we pass on a vision. We don't say it that way, but we do it all the time. A client and a builder undertake a project. The client must convey the vision they have in mind for the finished structure so the builder can complete the task to bring the vision to reality. We ask someone to pick something up for us at a store. We know exactly what the item looks like, and about where it is located. We convey the vision we have of the item and its location. The other person tries to get that same vision in mind so they can easily locate the item. Simplistic illustration, yes, but it is exactly what we are doing when we seek to witness for our Lord Jesus. We are trying to share the vision of the God of love that we know, and the beauty of the life He has planned for us. It become the work of God's Spirit working in the mind and heart of that other person so that they see the same vision we do. It is also what God has done with us by speaking through His Word to help us get the vision of all He is offering us in His life. When we begin to get that vision deeply in our own minds they we are able to build our life around it. Catching that vision leads to a changed life, joy, and worship.

Doing Without the Gadgets

There was an interesting letter in yesterday's paper. A young couple with two children made the decision to get along without most of their electronics. They gave up TV, smart phones, and tablets, limiting themselves only to flip phones. They said the results were all positive. They had more time together as a family. Husband and wife communication improved. The children spent a lot of time playing outside. All results were positive except one. Friends and neighbors started making caustic comments about their lifestyle. The letter said nothing about whether they were Christian or not, but that unimportant at the moment. What was likely happening was that others felt a bit of judgment against their own lifestyle. Christians have experienced this when someone knowing of their faith apologizes for cursing around them. I make no judgment about whether we should follow the couples example. But when a good value, as that in God's Word is held up, it becomes a standard against which our lives are measured. Against that perfect standard we all fall short. It is that judgment that drives us to Jesus. He alone is the one who removed that judgment, allowing us to stand in perfect righteousness before our Holy God.

Not Just n Attachment

When we send an e-mail we can add an attachment. It is usually something that is interesting or helpful. It's easy to do. A few clicks of the mouse and a document or a picture is added to the e-mail. Our problems in life comes when we treat God as an attachment. Many see God as interesting or helpful in certain situations, but otherwise off to the side and relatively unimportant to the task of getting along in life. But our God, revealed to us in Jesus Christ, must not be treated that way. Scripture, both Old and New Testaments picture man's relationship with God as that of the bride to the bridegroom. No bridegroom, no spouse, ever wants to be treated as an attachment. Our God calls us to be His bride. He knows us deeply, and has declared that He will never leave of forsake us. Our God cares about every situation, every choice, every action of life - of our lives. He will not be just an attachment. The more we understand God in the depth of the relationship He calls us to, the more we want to be a part of Him, and have Him a part of all we are and all we do.

Not The Last Word

We don't have to look far to know that we are in a broken world. The trials and pains of life come to all of us. It is how we deal with them that matters. And I must readily admit that I don't always deal with them in the right way. I am not a good patient when I face some pain. I took a fall last week that wrenched my back. It is painful when I move and have to use a walker to get around. I don't like not being able to get up and go. Which leads to frustration, etc. etc. etc. I said I'm not a good patient. I often wake up with the verse of some song playing in my mind. This morning it was a reminder that I needed. It was an Easter song highlighting the events of the cross and empty tomb. "Then came the morning."

> Then came the morning shadows
> vanished before the sun death had
> lost and life had won the morning
> had come.

This is the assurance we have. This is the message of the Gospel. God has come to share our burdens and to redeem us from the power of sin, death, and the devil. We have that assurance in the empty tomb. The morning has come, and with that truth we have the assurance that it will come for each us. I'm still not a good patient, but whatever I go through today is not the final word. My present pain will ease up, but more importantly we live the daily hope that in Christ all things shall be made new. Including our broken bodies.

New Lessons In Many Places

Paul wrote to the Roman Church that what can be know of God is clearly seen in the things God has made. It is always striking to me how that proves true in so many "normal" areas of life. I am currently in the hospital awaiting a hip replacement. That means a number of things. To go through with this I have to have trust in the skill of the surgeon and staff to do all that is right for my good. I have to trust the science behind their skills that it is correct and that they have learned it properly. And I have a choice. I can yield myself to them believing that what they do will bring healing and a better life to me. Think about that. Isn't that a picture of what God is asking us. I have to trust those who are bringing God's word to me, and that my best good is in their hearts. Further I have to trust the truth of God's Holy Word that it leads me to the fullness of life and joy. Then I have a choice. I can yield myself to the abundant grace that has already been provided for me and for all people, and find the cleansing and wholeness freely extended. Or I can refuse to yield and stay in the brokenness of my sinful self, the disease for which the cross is the only cure. So, you see that life around us has many lessons leading us to know our true God of life and hope.

God Works Through Various Means

I've written these messages from home which is where most of them come from. But technology as allowed my to write them when on vacation, traveling, and even now laying on my hospital bed. Computers and the internet have become a great tool in sharing our Lord's truth. (Along with many other things requiring us to use a great deal of discernment in how we use it.) So, technology has opened many doors, but that is not where the power of the Gospel lies. It is always in God, the Holy Spirit, who "called, gathers, enlightens, and sanctifies, as Luther said in the Small Catechism. I never claim that any of my messages are "from the Lord", but I do try to be faithful to His Word as best I understand it. I have receive many positive and useful comments over they years, but that is only because the Holy Spirit witnessed to some truth in the heart of the reader. No preacher ever saves anyone. It is the preacher's task to faithful share God's Word. It is the Holy Spirit to opens the heart of the hearer, causing them to yield to the gracious gift of life through Jesus Christ. When someone comes to faith it is the full Trinity, Father, Son, and Holy Spirit., who is involved,. We can only bow in humble thanksgiving to the One who loves us with an everlasting love.

THE LORD'S SENSE OF HUMOR

My most sincere thanks to all of you for your love and prayers. It is now 4:45AM. I am in my room and have slept for the past 7 hours. I am not in any discomfort except that my mouth is dry. I'm sorry to make this such a personal message. I don't like being at the center of attention, but there is a real witness to the Lord's goodness here. I love the Lord's sense of humor! On the wall facing my bed is a white board with the names of the nurses attending me, and the plan for the day. When I awoke a little while ago the very first name I saw was that of the Charge Nurse - JOY! God is so good. Not all circumstances or outcomes are good, but that doesn't change the goodness of our gracious Lord. "Rejoice in the Lord always. And again I will say rejoice." My love, and above all God's love to each of you dear readers. Stay blessed in the Lord Jesus Christ.

Just Believe in God?

It is not enough to believe in God. Many people say they do, but the concepts of God vary tremendously. James, the writer of the New Testament epistle, wrote that "You believe that there is one God. Good! Even the demons believe that--and shudder."[(James 2:19)] The concept of the God we believe in makes a huge difference in life. Is God near or far off? Is he involved in individual lives, or is He too busy? Does He know the depth of our hearts, or does He pretty much leave us alone? And what does it mean to say that He is holy? Scripture throughout shows us a God who is absolutely holy, and who calls us to be holy. He is a God who wants each and every person to know Him and be a part of Him. To understand His nature of pure sacrificial love, and to be a part of that love. This is the God who has revealed Himself in the person of Jesus Christ in order that we might find redemption and life through Him, that we might stand in His holy presence. This is not just any god as we might conceive him. He is a holy God who has done all that is necessary for us to have a true and abundant life in Him.

Life Is More Than A Number Of Years

Some scientists are working on technologies related to human longevity. Some have declared that Immortality may not be a reality yet, but rapidly evolving technology is making it more realistic. Scientists are expecting a tremendous transformation in health and medicine in the next 10 to 20 years. Honestly, I weep at such a report, and they are not tears of joy. It is absolute humanism and paganism akin to the Tower of Babel recorded in Genesis 11. It is a complete lack of understanding of both man and God. I am certainly not opposed to healing diseases, but the emphasis on human longevity denies the truth of our faith in Christ. In Jesus Christ we have the promise of eternal life in the Kingdom of God. Physical death is simply a step over into a perfect kingdom without sin. There is the key. Any human kingdom or society that men make will be one with the same fallen and corrupt natures, even if people have a 1000 years of life. All they gain is more time to exercise that corrupt nature. God calls us to life, true life in a relationship with Him through His Son, Jesus Christ. This is an unending life more beautiful than anything we could possible conceive.

Not Much Has Changed

Our Adult Bible class is currently looking at the Book of Psalms. The hundred and fifty Psalms were written more than 3000 years ago yet many of their expressions are as current as today's news. The human condition has not changed in all that time. We have the same needs, we commit the same sin, we find the same joys in life as then. But above all, and perhaps something we've grown dull to, they assumed that God was a part of all life. He heard their cries. He received their praise. They expected His intervention. Maybe that is why people love the Psalms. It shows a God who cares about the people He created, and has not left them alone. But then we have an even greater witness to this truth in the person of Jesus Christ, Almighty God come among us. He came to share all parts of human life, but even more. The Psalms testify to the only begotten Son of God who came to redeem mankind, defeating the power of sin, death, and the devil. Jesus is the assurance that God cares, that He is present, and the strength we need. God really is a part of all life.

It's Not about What I Don't Have

"Yet I will..." That is a phrase of choice, of determining to set one's mind and heart in a right direction. It is important for all of us in our relationship with our Lord. It is important for me where I presently reside in a rehabilitation center healing from a broken hip. Be assured I will not dwell on my injury for further Good Morning, but there are lessons for me to learn here, and these words from Habakkuk 3 are important. This is a nice place, but I don't like being here. Everything I did before automatically is now a chore, and tiring. I don't have the use of one of my limbs, but then my roommate has no use of all four of his. My inconvenience is minor for a week or so. He has been here for four months already. So I'm back to that choice. In spite of all this "Yet I will ... exalt in the Lord, I will rejoice in the God of my salvation." (Habakkuk 3:18) What is it we face in life? Sure it is tough. We live in a broken and sin filled world. We are all subject to the trials the fallen world contains. But there is One who has come to redeem the world from sin. His work is complete, and we have His promise that all tears will be wiped away and all sighing cease. It is our choice, we focus on the trial, or we focus on the strength His grace provides and hope of all that is yet to come. "Yet I will ..."

Being Fit In Soul And Body

In our small town there are several fitness centers and probably five or six rehilibition facilities. I don't think we are unusual. We hear a lot today about proper diet and exercise. Whether we actually follow all the proper guidance or not we know that this is the only way our bodies stay fit and strong. What goes into us is important, and how we use our bodies strengthens or weakens us. If this is true in the physical realm, it is equally true in the spiritual realm. To stay strong in our relationship and growth with the Lord we must have a regular diet of Holy Scripture, prayer, worship, and fellowship with other believers. We have heard in our country about the epidemic of obesity. The very opposite of fitness. Statistics have also shown that Biblical knowledge across the U.S. is very poor. We have become spiritually obese indulging in all manner of things except what really draws us closer to the One Person who really matters in life. Paul advising his spiritual son Timothy wrote, "Training the body has some value. But being godly has value in every way. It promises help for the life you are now living and the life to come."(1 Timothy 4:8) Let's get fit friends.

THE LORD, OUR ROCK

Many a sermon has begun with the words of Psalm 19 verse 14, "May these words of my mouth and this meditation of my heart be pleasing in your sight, LORD, my Rock and my Redeemer." It also seems to me that this prayer is a good way to begin each of our days. We will speak many words in a variety of situation throughout each day. Some in the context of our faith. Most in the normal secular activities of the day. Some well thought out for a specific task. Others, will be in casual conversation, or a spur of the moment response. The Lord is our Rock, the foundation of our lives. We desire that all that comes from us reflects the grace He extends to all people. That doesn't mean that everything we say is solemn and pious. Our Lord is a joy. All He did was for the good of others, and that is our desire. Whether our words must be hard in giving direction or correction, or if they are to please and build up another, or just plain good fun, our words build up and not pull down. May God's grace be upon you and undergird you in all you do today.

MIZPAH

Many years ago I was going on a trip away from my family. I received a greeting card from my uncle wishing me well, and it was simply signed Mizpah. I had heard the word but had to look it up again. It comes from the book of Genesis chapter 31, verse 49. It was a time when Jacob was leaving Laban, his father-in-law, taking all his family and possessions with him. The two men made a covenant between them marking it with a small stone monument. Jacob called that Mizpah. Well, what does a somewhat obscure Old Testament story have to do with my trip? Just this. The Hebrew word Mizpah means "The LORD watch between me and thee, when we are absent one from another." It was a beautiful expression of trust that the Lord would care for both until they could again be united. Not a bad way to sign a card when miles or circumstance separate separate us. Mizpah.

THIS MEANS THAT

In a conversation yesterday another man and I were talking about the value of imagination. When we were kids we made up all kinds of activities, characters, and games. We imagined what it would be like to be or to do this or that. Even the playing card we attached to the spokes of a bicycle making a motor sound took us to another place or time. God has given us the faculty of imagination to see beyond where we are at present. Jesus tried to guide His followers in this when He would say "the Kingdom of God is like...." Hewould give them an image of something they knew well, sheep, fields, merchants in search of some value, and so on, to help them see beyond this life into the nature of the place where God dwells, and where God desired that they be. Their imagination wasn't just for a child's game, but for a true image of all God held out our them. And as children take on a character they were being called to live in the nature of the Kingdom that was to come. This is still our calling. Scripture shows us the nature of our Lord and His life. By God's grace we are called and enabled to grow in that nature now. We bring the image of God's life into our everyday activities. It is this that draws other to Him.

GOD FORGETS

Getting older we tend to forget things and have trouble quickly recalling words or names. Our God, of course, has an infinite mind that forgets nothing. He knows all of our actions from first to last, the good and the bad. Yet, scripture assures us that "when we confess our sins He is faithful and just to forgive our sins and cleanse us from all unrighteousness.[1 John 1:9] In His divine grace Isaiah tell us that "you have put all my sins behind your back."[Isaiah 38:17] Think of the magnitude of what our gracious Lord is doing."Though your sins are like scarlet, they shall be as white as snow; though they are red as crimson, they shall be like wool."[Isaiah 1:18] In our time of confession in our Sunday worship I am allowed to say, by Christ's command, "I declare unto you the entire forgiveness of all your sins." The magnitude of that statement is beyond measure. By the blood shed on Calvary our sins, all of them, are cleansed and we are allowed to stand before our Holy God having the righteousness of our Lord Jesus Christ. No, God doesn't forget, but He forgives - and that is supremely more valuable.

WEDDING VOWS

Over the years I've done quite a few weddings. Couples come with a variety of desires and expectations. If I'm not familiar with the couple the first question I usually ask is why do they want a pastor to do their wedding, and why in the church? I usually get a variety of answers with few having anything to do with the real reason they should seek a church wedding. And then there is the business of couples wanting to write their own wedding vows. That doesn't go over too well either. Too often couples treat the wedding service like another part of the beautiful decorations for the day. It's all a big beautiful party. But it isn't. Marriage is one of the most serious commitments we make in life. If we want it to last "till death us do part" then it must be done in the way God designed it. Years ago there was a TV program called Father Knows Best. In the case of weddings our Father really does know best. After explaining all this at the beginning of a counseling session I've had one or two couple walk away and go somewhere else, and that's OK. We need to understand the seriousness of the relationship we enter. Only then can it grow into the beauty of the male/female bond as God intended.

A Glimpse Of The Kingdom

Many of Jesus' parables began "the Kingdom of God is like." He took Peter, James, and John up with Him on the mount of Transfiguration where they saw Moses and Elijah, and heard the voice of God. He wanted His followers to understand that there was a real life beyond what there five senses could detect. And it was not just some place with clouds, harps, angels, and spirits floating around. It would ultimately be a new heaven and a new earth where righteousness dwells. He wanted them to understand the truth, and the values of that life because that is what they were to bring now into this life. And so it is to be with us. We live now motivated and guided by all that we know is yet to come. We seek to bring as much of Kingdom life into the service of our world as we can. That applies whether it is our continuing contacts with a neighbor, a matter of doing justice in a small local situation, or our attitudes and opportunities we have in larger spheres. As Jesus taught of the Kingdom, others are to see a small glimpse of that Kingdom in us. It is real.

To Be Complete

A young man came to Jesus one day asking about how he could inherit eternal life. Jesus spoke to him about keeping the commandments which the man said that he had always tried to do. Jesus responded, "If you would be complete sell your possessions, give to the poor, and come follow me". (Matthew 19:21) The young man went away sad because he was very wealthy. There is much we could say about this encounter, but what stood out to me about this passage were Jesus' words, "if you would be complete" or be perfect in other translations. Our salvation is complete. It is a totally finished act of God's grace in Jesus on Calvary. We do nothing to make it any more complete, yet do we want it? Or are we more content with our own will, our own ways, our own desires? God holds out a Kingdom to us, as we wrote about yesterday, but we can refuse to yield to his gift. It is like someone given a beautifully wrapped present. It is totally theirs, but if they refuse to unwrap it the treasure inside is of little use. Keep your heart set on that treasure, the righteousness of Christ won for you at the cross. You will grow more into it day by day as the Lord makes you complete.

TRUE WORSHIP

What brings you to worship? Worship is more than going to church on a Sunday morning. That is certainly important, but worship is the attitude of the heart that bows humbly before the awe, the wonder, the majesty of the God who created us. It is as expressed in Psalm 8. "When I consider Your heavens, the work of Your fingers, The moon and the stars, which You have ordained; What is man that You take thought of him, And the son of man that You care for him?" (Psalm 8:3-4) I ask again, what brings you to worship? What do you see with your heart that draws you into the Holy Presence at the Throne of Grace? It may be the grandure of the Hallelujah Chorus. It may be the breathtaking beauty of something in nature. It may be the wonder of a God, our God, who came as the Bethlehem baby. Whatever it is, it is that which brings us into the building we call a church to sing, to pray, to hear God's word, and to kneel at the altar hearing the words "given and shed for you for the forgiveness of your sins". We don't go to church to worship. We bring worship into the church joining humbly with others before the majesty of our God.

THE DESIGNER

I have had numerous occasions to fly in an airplane over the years. There is not much to do while seated in a rather cramped seat but to read, sleep, or stare out of the window. I usually do all of these on any flight. It is the staring out of the window part that often catches my attention. Looking at an airplane wing one sees the various parts and how it was constructed. Mechanical things always fascinate me. I notice the rivets on the wing's surface. They are in a very specific pattern. Two parallel rows, four rivets pointing forward, then the two rows took a distinct 30 degree angle going on for another ten or so rivets. I have no idea why, but obviously an aircraft design engineer found a very specific need to place them that way. I can say I'm thankful for that, because it is part of what was gets me to my destination. Just the thoughts of an idle mind during a flight? Perhaps, but the intentionality of the pattern means the presence of a very real designer. But then go back one step further, thinking about the mind of that designer. Intricate and more complex than anything in this craft that holds me up at 38,000 feet. That mind had to have a Designer infinitely smarter than any collection of engineers that put this plane together. Paul wrote that "what can be known about God is clearly visible in the things God has made."(Romans 1:20) For that Designer I am even more thankful.

Good To Come Home

Our local paper always has a short saying at the bottom of the front page by some famous person. The one yesterday said that is doesn't matter where one lives in the world or what their culture it is always good to come home after being away. How true. I've just come home after three weeks in the hospital and rehab facility. How good it is to be here. We've all experienced this when coming home from a vacation, no matter how good a time we've had. This seems to be a universal longing to get back to where we belong. I think this universal longing also points to something deeper. We all have a longing to get back to Eden, to the true and pure place of our relationship with our Lord. I've written this week about Jesus' parables of the Kingdom. That is our true home. That is what all of our other longings and desires point to. But it is also what we seek to bring into this present world, at least in many small ways, by our life in Jesus Christ lived for the good of others.

Full of Hypocrites?

We sometimes hear the charge from those outside of the church that the church is full of hypocrites. That's why they don't want to be a part of it. Well, actually the charge is true. The church does have hypocrites in it, as well as all other kinds of sinners that one finds anywhere else in the world. The difference is that those in the church know where they can find forgiveness and new life. Jesus lived and taught among sinners in order to provide for them a better way of life. Do we in the church still sin? Of course we do. We are no better than anyone else, but we do know who is the source of all life, and we do desire to grow closer to Him. So we in the church are not telling outsiders that they are more evil than we are. We are inviting them to come share with us on a journey toward something far better than anything the world can offer.

Love Songs

A number of the old Gospel songs talk about our relationship with the Lord. "He walks with me and the talks with me and He tells me I am His own.", ... "I am His and His is mine and His banner over me is love.", are just a couple of the lines. They tend to be sentimental and not always the best theology, but they do speak of a relationship that that is deep and on going. The Lord can't be contained in the hour we worship on Sunday morning. We certainly need that hour of fellowship and support from other believers and to be fed by God's word and the Holy Sacrament. But the Lord is just as real and present on Monday and Tuesday mornings as on Sundays. That's what the old songs are trying to say. They are love song to our Bridegroom. Earthly love songs also tend to be sentimental, but they recognize that we are never apart from the relationship with the beloved . So if you were in church yesterday, recognize that the same Lord you worshiped then is with you today. His desire is to draw you ever closer to Himself and help you grow in His life.

Food For Life

The disciples returned to Jesus on one occasion bringing lunch for their group. They urged Jesus to eat. He responded, "I have food to eat that you know nothing about ".(John 4:32) They didn't understand at the time, but He was speaking of spiritual food that sustains one's whole being. Certainly we need physical food, but without spiritual food the physical food ultimately does us little good. I'm sure you have gathered from my writing that I'm a sacramental Christian. By that I mean that the sacraments we share in the context of our worship are very important to me. The sacraments of baptism and the Lord's Supper are very real and present gifts of God's grace. They are not simply symbols or remembrances of things that happened 2000 year ago. When we come to worship we are fed by hearing God's Word and by receiving the true Body and Blood of Jesus in the communion. These are cleansing and life sustaining acts of God's grace. This is true food for our spiritual being.

EXPRESSING OUR JOY

People have their favorite sports teams they root for. I'm always interested to watch the fans at these events. Fans will do the most outrageous things to support their team. Painted faces, strange wigs, and other head gear, hold up signs, and wave banners, all manner of jumping, arm waving, and shouting. The excitement over a good play pours out of the crowd. I wonder why we can't get that excited about the things of the Lord. We don't have to paint our faces and put on funny hats, but when we realize all that the Lord has done for each of us, it should bring a thrill to our hearts, an expressions of praise to our lips. "Oh! but we are in church. We have to be dignified." Jesus got excited. When the disciples came back from their mission to the towns of Israel reporting all that had happened. The text says, "At that time Jesus, full of joy through the Holy Spirit," prayed... The word translated "full of joy" really means "jumped for joy". He saw his people beginning to take hold of God's truth, and was excited. We do things "decently and in order" in church, but raise your hands once in a while in praise. When you have a chance to pray aloud, let the expressions of your heart glorify God. No football fan should have anything on us. We have the greatest God of all!

TRUE ARMOR

Research and technology do a great deal to protect those in our armed services. We've made body armor, vehicles to withstand road side bombs, and all manner of high tech equipment. This is all necessary for the safety of our troops, as best as we can protect them. There is an even greater protection that we all need for our daily lives. It's called "the full armor of God". We really are in a daily spiritual warfare, battling things that would pull us away from the values that honor our Lord. We are told in Ephesians to, "Stand firm then, with the belt of truth buckled around your waist, with the breastplate of righteousness in place, and with your feet fitted with the readiness that comes from the gospel of peace. In addition to all this, take up the shield of faith, with which you can extinguish all the flaming arrows of the evil one. Take the helmet of salvation and the sword of the Spirit, which is the word of God." (Ephesians 6:14-17) Truth, righteousness, peace, faith, and salvation - these are very real strengths we possess from the grace of God. They must not be neglected. We have only one offensive weapon - the Word of God. That above all must be with us daily. Together, this is a protection greater than anything our technologies can make.

A PRAYER FOR YOUR DAY

Gracious Lord God, You have created mankind and all that is. The heavens declare Your glory, and all the earth shows Your handiwork. The mark of Your life is upon all that exists. And You have made me. You knew me before I was born, and created me for Your good purpose. I have not always sought to know that purpose, or follow it when I did. Forgive me, Good Lord. Yet, You have redeemed me through Christ Jesus, and because of Him I can always be restored again to Your grace. You have given me each breath that I take, and You have given me spiritual breath by the presence of Your Holy Spirit. You continue to guide my life, and give me strength for every situation. You have given me family and friends, and material blessings beyond anything I deserve or could earn. For all of this, Good Lord, I am forever grateful. My desire is to come ever closer to You, and to give you thanks and praise for all eternity. To You be glory and honor, now and forever, through Christ Jesus my Lord. Amen.

THE OFFENSE OF THE CROSS

We often see the cross worn as a piece of jewelry. I have a number of cross lapel pins. Military cemeteries will have row upon row of white cross grave markers. It is a prominent symbol, and sometimes one wonders what it means to the one wearing it? Because at its core the cross is offensive. The cross confronts us with our sin and our separation from Almighty God. It shows us who we really are, and that we are incapable of making ourselves acceptable. The cross strikes us at the very core of our pride, and humbles us before the God by whom we were created. The cross also confronts us with the overwhelming grace of God who did something for us that we are incapable of doing for ourselves in making atonement for our sins . This is why crosses are torn down by persecutors of our faith. Yet, when we really understand the meaning of the cross, and wear it knowing the gift of life we've been given, we can joyfully sing the words of the Gospel song "So I'll cherish the old rugged Cross Till my trophies, at last, I lay down I will cling to the old rugged Cross And exchange it some day for a crown."

Your Self Image

We are told that having a positive self image is important. It affects all we do in life. We have confidence in ourselves when we undertake a project. Teachers try to build this in their students. But perhaps it would be better to build the God image in people. For in that we were created. What greater image can we have than knowing we are God's child through faith in Jesus Christ. Almighty God knew us from before we were born. He created us. He has called us into an eternal relationship with Himself, and made that possible through the sacrifice of Jesus, His Son. There is no greater self image than knowing that we are God's child for Jesus sake. This doesn't puff us up with pride because it is nothing we have done. It is what we have been given. If we begin teaching this to our children from their earliest age they grow with a confidence, not in themselves, but in God. God has given each of us certain talents and abilities. We can use them with confidence for the Glory of God and for the good of others. Go about your tasks today knowing that Almighty God has made you and called you to be in eternal fellowship with Himself. Do your best in all you do and let God's love shine in your life.

A Spiritual Discipline

How do you read the Bible? Do you start at the beginning of one book and work your way progressively through? Or do you let the Bible fall open and read whatever you find there? Not recommended, though I've tried it at times. Reading the Bible is a discipline one cultivates. And here I have to be honest and say I've not always done so. It is far too easy to let it slip in the press of other things. Yet it is important for the whole direction of our lives. There is a wonderful verse in Psalm 119. "Your word is a lamp for my feet, a light on my path."(Psalm 119:105) The image is real. Walking in darkness it is easy to stumble and fall. We need a light for our path. The light of God's Word is of supreme value in walking through this dark world. It is what make sense of the things we see. Let's work on that habit of the daily reading of Scripture.

TO SEE WITH GOD'S LOVE

One of the hardest things I've had to do in recovering from my hip surgery is to slow down. But I'm used to getting things done, mentally listing my accomplishments at the end of the day. So slowing down is hard. But there is another aspect to slowing down. A while back I heard a prayer, a rather simple one, "Lord, help me to see all people with the same love as You see them." Such a request should be taken fore granted, should it not? After all isn't that what Christians are supposed to do? Yes. But when I consider myself I very clearly don't do this all the time. I'm in a hurry, I make quick judgments by outward appearances, size, manners, speech, skin color, and a host of other features. My Christian training tells me that each person is one for whom Christ gave his life, but do I really care? I'm busy, got things to do, a schedule to keep. So I think the Lord impressed this prayer upon me again. Lord, help me to see all people with the same love as You see them. Slow down. Don't make those quick superficial judgments. Even consider a quick prayer of blessing for them. - I'll try Lord, but continue to work Your grace in me to cleanse out what is not of You, and above all I bow in humble thanks for the mercy of forgiving grace in Jesus Christ. - So slowing down can be helpful in a lot of ways.

CHOOSE THIS DAY

Toward the end of Joshua's life he gathered the people of Israel and challenged them, Choose this day whom you will serve...the pagan gods of the nations around you or the one true God of Israel. (Joshua 24:15) Many years later Elijah stood on Mt. Carmel and asked the people "How long will you waver between two opinions? If the Lord is God follow him, but if Baal is god, follow him." (1Kings 18:21) This is the question that comes down through all the centuries since creation. The Lord God has revealed Himself to mankind in many ways, but we live in a world of many competing voices all seeking our allegiance. Who do we serve? Jesus asked His disciples one day, "Who do people say that I am?". They gave him a variety of answers that they had heard. But then Jesus asked them directly, "But what about you? Who do you say that I am?" Peter answered, "You are the Christ, the Son of the living God." (Matthew 16:16) This question comes to us and is of ultimate importance for life. The answer we give is the difference between living in a world of confusion, questions and contradictions, or a world that begins to make sense because the Living God has chosen to occupy this life with us. Who do you say that I am?

OUR ROCK IN ALL TIMES

"I love you, O LORD, my strength. The LORD is my rock, my fortress and my deliverer; my God is my rock, in whom I take refuge. He is my shield and the horn of my salvation, my stronghold. I call to the LORD, who is worthy of praise, and I am saved from my enemies." David gives us a wonderful prayer of trust in this Psalm. He is clear in saying that life is a struggle. There [Psalm 18:1-3] are many battles and enemies to the point where he feels overwhelmed, but the Lord is always there, bringing him through to life. This is our trust in all times, and all conditions. Life in our fallen world is not easy. There are many things that try to separate us from our trust in the Lord. Circumstances don't turn out as we would like, or even as we can understand. Yet, God is there. He is our rock, our fortress, and our deliverer. He is worthy of our praise in all times, and our praise turn the eyes of our heart to Him.

MUST WE HATE?

The report came out a day or so ago that the number of so called hate groups in the U.S. has increased markedly. I think the number they said was around a thousand. These are groups strongly opposed to a particular race or ideology and at times use drastic physical means to oppose them. Unfortunately the Church is sometimes wrongly lumped into these groups. It is true that some Christian people have used drastic means to oppose certain things, but these should be condemned along with all the rest who use force, violence, and intimidation for their cause. The Church does oppose certain actions or behaviors, abortion for example. But it is to use education and other peaceful means. The Church's mandate is to love all people. Our desire is for all people to have the best life the Lord gives. We do not, should not, hate anyone. It was Jesus who ate with us sinners and wanted wholeness for us all. So it must be with His Church.

Life Is Complicated

I've been reading again the Old Testaments accounts of the various kings of Judah and Israel. There was a very simple formula repeated over and over. If they followed the ways of the Lord they prospered. Their armies succeed, their crops did well, they had food, and there was generally peace and prosperity. When they did not follow the Lord the very opposite happened until the nations itself was destroyed. In many ways that formula has always been true whether for nations or for individuals. I know we then get into the discussion about, why we see good people suffering. We also know that we live under the grace of our Lord Jesus Christ and not under the Law. Life is complicated, and we don't understand all the ways our Lord chooses to work with us. But that doesn't change the basic formula for life. In His holy Word he has given us a way of life that is for our good. If we come before God in humility, in repentance for our sinfulness, and truly desire to understand and live by all God has said for good, then we do have peace and prosperity. We don't do it for that reason, we do it because we have been called into a personal relationship with our Lord who loves us deeply and we love Him in return. It doesn't mean that we will never have problems or suffer, but even in the midst of difficulties our peace remains and we can trust the Lord to bring all things to their right conclusion."The counsel of the LORD stands forever, The plans of His heart from generation to generation. Blessed is the nation whose God is the LORD, The people whom He has chosen for His own inheritance." (Psalm 33:11-12)

In What Is Our Fulfillment?

People go to all kinds of lengths for excitement and challenges. A record has been set for the most bungy jumps is a short period of time, also for the number of back flips across a football field. Certainly not something I ever would have considered trying. Even so it highlight something in our nature that craves a challenge, that thrives on excitement, and that desires to be singled out for a good accomplishment. Being a part of the nature God created, these desires are not wrong. The problem with so much of mankind is that we seek fulfillment in the wrong places. The Lord offers us all of these in His service. If you read the Gospels, the life Jesus is offering His followers is a constant challenge. A life of faith comes with no guarantees for an easy time, and without any knowledge of what is ahead. We enter a walk with the Lord where His central instruction simply says "trust Me". From here He takes us in directions we never dreamed, but if we are willing to follow His path we will hear the only commendation that really matters, "Well done good and faithful servant.".

THE POWER OF LOVE

What is powerful? Nations will talk about their military might. Others may speak of heavy equipment that moves earth or lifts massive weights. We might think of tornadoes, hurricanes, or flood waters. All of these certainly are powerful. However, yesterday I experienced again the most power force on earth or in heaven. The power of love. Yesterday was the final service I conducted at my congregation, followed by a wonderful luncheon. The church was full of dear members, family, and friends. Emotion was certainly there, but the power was the power of love, of God's love, that enfolded and bound each of us together as one. All other powers are simply forces that work on the outside of a person for good or ill. Love changes hearts and shapes lives at the deepest part of ones being. Jesus had changed all of us who were gathered, as He has changed countless lives through two thousand years since He walked this land. People search for love in many places, but too often find only poor counterfeits or pain. Our God is love, and He is continually extending Himself to us. The shed blood on Calvary's cross is the most powerful, life-giving, loving act there is. And it was given and shed for you. Come.

REAL TRUTHS IN SCRIPTURE

The Tabernacle was the worship center that the people of Israel carried along with them on their journey out of Egypt on their way to the Promised Land. God gave Moses the extremely detailed plan for the Tabernacle when he was on Mt. Sinai. The detail was so great that it takes about 16 chapter of the Old Testament to fully describe it. Reading it seems tedious, and rather useless for us, but it really is not. Even as Jesus told many parables pointing to truths that were far deeper, so the things that God establishes are intended to teach and ultimately to bring us nearer to Himself. The Apostle Paul wrote, "For since the creation of the world His invisible attributes, His eternal power and divine nature, have been clearly seen, being understood through what has been made,..."(Romans 1:20) This challenges us to observe, to think, and to pray. From marriage and family, to the natural world around us, to a look into the cosmos, it is all touched by God's hand and speaks of things that help to understand Him more fully. Oh the wideness of God's grace and the depth of His love!

A Different Path

In reading through the Old Testament we see God's call to Noah, Abraham, and Moses to a task He had for them. In each case they were called to come out of a pagan culture, listen to and be obedient to God, and lead their people into a different way of life. We could also look at the whole nation of Israel, for that was their calling as well. In fact, that is the definition of what Christ's church is to be - people called out to live a different life in obedience to our Lord. It is not that we are better than anyone else. We are all sinful by nature, but we have been shown a better way of life in harmony with God. The problem with the church today is that, by many measures, it is not distinguishable from the surrounding culture. The walk of each of the Old Testament figures, and in fact for all of us, begins with hearing the call of our Lord to come and follow Him. He has given us His Holy Word both as a declaration of His redeeming love and as a guide in living a life pleasing to Him. It is that life that is to be a witness to the world and draw others to Him.

Do We Think Like Jacob?

There is an account in Genesis 28 of the patriarch Jacob traveling toward his ancestral home in Haran. He spends a night out in open country and has a dream in which God blesses him. Upon awakening he is amazed, declares the place to be the House of God, and makes a vow. He says, "If God will be with me and will watch over me on this journey I am taking and will give me food to eat and clothes to wear so that I return safely to my father's house, then the LORD will be my God."(Genesis 28:20-21) It really is a terrible vow. He is telling God that you must do this, this, and this for me if you want me to follow you. But I wonder if that is not also the thinking behind the modern day question of how could a good God allow such and such a tragedy to happen? We expect God to bless us. We put parameters around what we think is a blessing. But we are dealing with a sovereign God, a God who see life far beyond our meager view. We are also dealing with a God, our God, who has both declared and demonstrated His love for us in Jesus Christ. He is working for the good of His creation, and for our good, far beyond our capacity to understand. "In quietness and trust is our strength."(Isaiah 30:15)

St. Valentine

Valentine's Day, or properly St. Valentine's Day, has become a day emphasizing romantic love with flowers and gifts for sale in many of our stores. The romantic love between a man and a woman is a wonderful gift of God. However, it is not the deepest form of love, but only one form pointing to something far deeper. St. Valentine has unfortunately become submerged under all of the flowers and chocolates. St. Valentine was a third century priest in Rome who worked to help many Christians who were being persecuted at that time. His efforts finally cost him his own life. Jesus has said "no greater love has any man than this that he lay down his life for his friend". [John 15:13] This is the true self sacrificing love of God. It is the love that St. Valentine showed toward those he served. It is also the love that makes romantic love truly complete.

Don't Put God In A Box

In Mark chapter 6 Jesus returns to His home town. He had the opportunity to teach the people, many of whom were His former neighbor, friends, or perhaps people He had done work for in the carpenter's shop. Their response to His message - "Where did this fellow get this stuff?" (My free translation!) This was the carpenter's son after all. We know his family. Where is this wisdom coming from? It was as if there was a darkness, a blanket over the eyes of their hearts. They couldn't or wouldn't let themselves trust what He was saying. That just seems so contemporary to me. We, particularly Americans, but the modern Western world in general, are so set in our own cultural norms, our technological mind set, all dulled by the pursuit of pleasure that our own eyes become darkened to spiritual truth. The god many believe in has to fit within the boxes they've made. When some preacher tries to say there's more, there's something deeper, there is a different way of life, the same response comes. Where did he get this stuff? But "this stuff" is very real and a truth the Lord want to open for all people. There really is much more to life than what our limited senses take in.

Lost By The Digital World

In the corner of my office I have a floor to ceiling bookcase. There are seven shelves holding a few hundred books. Everything on those shelved could be contained within some number of megabytes on one of the new tablet devices. A book would be instantly available by a touch of the finger, and pages turned by the swipe of a hand. It would free up a number of square feet of floor space. Convenient, yes. Part of the wonders of our digital world, but I think of what would be lost. Those volumes have been collected over many years, from many different situations and needs. Some are gifts from people who are important to me; some signed and dated. I look at each shelf, I know what it contains and where I can find what I need. The very top of the shelf holds four wedding picture of couples I've married. They too could be in the digital file, along with thousands of others. The digital world is here to stay, and in many ways is very helpful, but as with all technological advances we also need to be careful what we lose by its use. God created man for relationship, first with Himself, then with others, and with all aspect of His created world. We should not let any technology harm that.

Humble, Lowly, and Meek

At one time Jesus prayed, "I praise you, Father, Lord of heaven and earth, because you have hidden these things from the wise and learned, and revealed them to little children. Yes, Father, for this was you good pleasure."(Luke 10:21) Jesus was always reversing things. The world exalts the powerful. Jesus looked to the weak. The world regards the wealthy and accomplished. Jesus looked to the poor and humble. The world wants to be with the respectable. Jesus spent His time with the sinners. Who was right? Was Jesus missing something? In the beginning of his ministry the devil tempted Jesus with all the glory of the worlds kingdoms, and with a spectacular miracle that would make many believe in Him. He rejected both. (Matthew 4:8-10) Yet He is the One to whom Scripture tell us that "every knee will bow, of those who are in heaven and on earth and under the earth, and every tongue confess that Jesus Christ is Lord, to the glory of God the Father."(Philippians 2:10-11) No, Jesus was not wrong in the company He kept, and it is a lesson for us in the ones we look up to in this world.

GOD WORKS IN THE EVENTS

A crowd had gathered around. Jesus had cast out a demon from a young boy that had seemed incurable. In Luke 9:43 it say, "And they were all amazed at the greatness of God." The comment by St. Luke made me wonder if at times we don't sell God a bit short? Did the crowd think that God was unable to do this healing? Yesterday's church service was the ordination and installation of the new Pastor for Christ Lutheran Church. Before the service a couple of us were standing in the hallway talking about the events that led up to this day. We could look back several years and see things that were put into place that made this day possible. God's hand had been and was at work in a number of lives to bring us to this time. God is able. Perhaps we look in the wrong places when we think that nothing is happening in answer to our prayers. God is present. He knows our deepest needs. He is more than able to provide. God knows the picture He is painting. For us it looks like pieces of a puzzle being fitted together. And when we begin to see the image we are called not to amazement, but to worship. Rejoice in your Lord who is working in your life according to His good purpose.

A Life That Praises God

Churches have praise teams to lead in congregational singing. We have prayer and praise services. Scripture speaks of praise to the Lord over 300 times. God speaking through Isaiah said, "... my people, my chosen, the people I formed for myself that they may proclaim my praise."(Isaiah 43:21) It can almost sound like God is an egotist demanding praise of His people, but this is the farthest from the truth. He is certainly worthy of our praise for all that He is, and all that He has done. God doesn't need our praise, but we need to praise. In praise we draw near to our Lord who is the source of our life. In praise we find our identity as children of our Heavenly Father. In praise our eyes are turned from the trials of life to the source of our strength. No, God doesn't need our praise, but He knows that as we come to Him in praise we are open to His life, and in His life we find life.

THE CURE

On March 26, 1953 Dr. Jonas Salk announced the discovery of the vaccine for polio. I was 13 at the time and polio was a greatly feared disease. We saw picture of children having to live in an iron lung just so they could breath. 1952 had been an epidemic year with 58,000 new cases, and 3,000 deaths. Dr. Salk was hailed as a hero, and since his time polio has pretty much become a thing of the past. Today is Ash Wednesday with many receiving the mark of the ashes on their foreheads, a reminder of the depth of our sinful nature before God. I begin with the story of polio to point out that the value of the cure is in proportion to the seriousness of the disease. Ash Wednesday reminds us that we all have a deadly serious disease, far more serious than polio. The disease is sin. "For all have sinned", wrote St. Paul, "and fall short of the glory of God". (Romans 3:23) Life is not a matter of just trying to do the best we can. It is not that we are pretty good and there are a lot of others worse than we are. The ashes reminded us that we all fall short of the only true standard for all life - God's perfect and eternal glory. The ashes are placed in the sign of the cross reminding us that the only true remedy for our deadly disease is the atoning sacrifice of Jesus Christ, our Savior. Don't ever lose sight of what the ashes represent, the deadly seriousness of our sin. For if we lose sight of that we also diminish the value of our Savior. The grace of God shown to us in the sacrifice of Christ is of value beyond measure.

WHERE OUR HOPE LIES

It is mid March. The temperature is still below freezing. The trees are still bare. The grass is brown. Yet we know that in a few short weeks things will begin to change. Buds will start to appear. The grass will start to grow. Spring flowers will come. We live in the anticipation of the warmth and beauty that is ahead. There is an even greater prospect in which Christians live. The Apostle Peter wrote, "fix your hope completely on the grace to be brought to you at the revelation of Jesus Christ."(1Peter 1:13) Many aspects of the world around us can look pretty barren, but we live in the truth that this is not all there is. Our Lord created us and He will bring all things to their right conclusion at the coming again of the Christ. This is not a pie in the sky vague hope, but a truth resting on the promises of our God. Whether He comes in our lifetime (for which we should daily pray) or afterward, the promise is sure just as we can be sure of spring. This hope changes our attitude about many things. It deepens our prayers for all those we care about. It gives us the desire to serve others, and help them to see the hope we have in the Lord. It's March, but April is coming, and so is the visible presence of our Lord Jesus. Our hope is in His grace.

Windows Into The Kingdom

When a person see a beautiful sight we sometimes hear the expression "it is breathtaking". There is a sense of awe and wonder concerning the experience. I have a CD recording of Mozart's Ave Verum that I will sometimes play through my computer while I'm working. I don't understand the words of the composition but the music and vocals are wonderful. I've been in groups of Christians singing a majestic hymn of our faith. At times its beauty has been so great I've had to stop singing and let the sound surround me with its wonder. I hope you can identify with this in one form or another. It is more than an emotional experience. It is being enveloped in a beauty beyond words. We can't live in those experiences continually while on earth, but I think they are windows that God gives us for a brief look into the Glory of His kingdom. This is a small glimpse into the glory that awaits all who are in Christ Jesus.

LORD, OPEN THE EYES OF OUR HEARTS

Paul writing to the Ephesian church said, "I keep asking that the God of our Lord Jesus Christ, the glorious Father, may give you the Spirit of wisdom and revelation, so that you may know him better. I pray also that the eyes of your heart may be enlightened in order that you may know the hope to which he has called you, the riches of his glorious inheritance in the saints, and his incomparably great power for us who believe."(Ephesians1:17-19) I can say this is also my prayer for all of you. It is really a prayer that I pray for myself as well. That the eyes of our hearts might be opened more and more to the real presence of God working in our daily lives. We do not serve a God who is far off or unconcerned. He is God with us, God of wisdom and strength sufficient for all of our needs. He is God at hand to be worshiped and praised. He is our redeeming God who has called us to Himself. May the eyes of your heart be opened more and more to see Him.

Meeting The Imperfections Of Life

This is not a perfect world. Nor are the things in our personal lives perfect. Boards for a project are not always flat. Kids don't always behave. Things get put away in the wrong places. Computers crash, and you can add to the list of irritating imperfections. The problem is we want things to be perfect. We don't want to deal with the irritations. It's frustrating. But it is what it is, and our frustrations are not going to make things perfect. The only way to meet the imperfections of life is with a nature that is perfect. The only perfect nature is that which God, the Holy Spirit, works within us, that of "love, joy, peace, forbearance, kindness, goodness, faithfulness, gentleness and self-control."(Galatians 5:22-23) Of course, we don't live in these attributes perfectly either, but think about it. If we were to meet the trials of life with more of these perfect characteristics, they would have a real power to change the present situation into something just a bit more perfect.

DON'T TEMPT THE LORD

A number of times the Jewish leaders tested Jesus with questions about taxes, or about marriage trying to get Him to say something they could use against Him. There is an Old Testament account about Gideon's fleece where Gideon was called to do a task for the Lord and on two consecutive days put a test before God to be sure he had heard the instructions correctly. This was also one of the temptations Satan put before Jesus asking Him to test God to prove He really was His Son. It was the very first temptation the devil put before Eve, "Did God really say...." Our Lord is not to be tested, but trusted. He has give us His Holy Word. It is why we have so often emphasized daily reading the Bible. It is by this that we know what is true, and it is by this that we test, not God, but all the things that come to us in the world. "For the word of God is living and active and sharper than any two-edged sword, able to judge the thoughts and intentions of the heart." (Hebrews 4:12)

On Lord, One Faith

In the early days of the Church after Pentecost there was a unity in Christ that bound all the believers together. It says of that time "all those who had believed were together and had all things in common". [Acts 2:44] Individuals sold their property and lived as a common community sharing all they had. This is not a model for the Church to continue, but what was important was the unity they had with one another in their common faith. Paul emphasizes this to the Corinthian Church in describing them in terms of a human body each part being essential to all the rest. [1 Corinthians 12] Tragically today we are divided into thousands of Christian denominations, and that unity is sometimes hard to see. What was central to that early Church was their common faith in the Lord Jesus Christ, and their devotion to the Holy Scripture. Where we can share that commonality today we can support and need to support one another. We will argue about different doctrines, but wherever we can we must support one another in our common faith in Jesus, the Christ.

TRUTH WORTH DYING FOR

We sometimes describe people as being open minded or close minded; willing to listen to other positions, or refusing to hear any other. Some Christians are accused of being closed minded fundamentalists condemning others, and there certainly are these, unfortunately. But the question is not how strictly one holds to a position, but how they seeks to share that position. For Christians, the divinity of Christ, and salvation by faith in Him are central. These truths cannot be given up, and are worth dying for. But how we share them is of prime importance. They are first shared by a life that is lived in sacrificial service. It is only the love of Christ through us that will draw others to Him. It is being open to others, and allowing them to see that we care, that will show them there is something better in Jesus. Christianity is a faith worth dying for, but more importantly it is a faith worth living to the fullest.

More To Life Than Feeling Good

Do you feel good today? I hope so. It's nice to feel good, but we have become a society that strives to always feel good. We expect our doctors to make us feel good. We look to our politicians to give us what we need to feel good. Teachers want students to feel good about themselves, and even some churches advertise that they make people feel good about coming. God never promised that we would always feel good. Certainly, there is nothing spiritual about feeling bad. That is not the point. But nowhere does God give us a promise that we would always feel good. He does, however, promise that He will never leave or forsake us; that His strength and grace are sufficient for all our needs; and that we can have His peace and joy regardless of our circumstances. That is a far better promise than just making us feel good.

CAN JESUS BE TOO MUCH?

In the eighth chapter of St. Matthew there is the account of Jesus' encounter with two demon possessed men. The demons, of course, recognized Him and begged to be sent into a nearby heard of swine when He cast them out. He did, and the swine rushed down the hillside and were drowned. When the town's people heard of it, rather than rejoicing over the healing of the two men, and bring others to be healed as happened elsewhere, they begged Jesus to leave their district. Sometimes Jesus is too much! He is too disturbing of our way of life. People get caught up in their own plans, their own lifestyle. Jesus just upsets too much. It doesn't make sense. This is why Jesus was always looking for humility, and the trusting faith of a child. Ones who were willing to put themselves in His hands even when it was disturbing and didn't make sense. "To all who did receive him, to those who believed in his name, he gave the right to become children of God."[(John 1:12)] And that really is far better than anything we might let stand in the way.

Losing Our Life

A Christian often finds himself caught in the middle - wanting to show compassion but needing to stand firm on convictions; facing battles in this world but without using the same weapons the world uses. The life of loving an enemy, turning the other cheek, and washing smelly feet is not an easy one. We are called to loose our life for Christ's sake in order to find it. This requires a complete change of heart which only God can accomplish within us. The Psalmist prayed, "Teach me your way, O Lord, and I will walk in your truth; give me an undivided heart, that I may fear your name." (Psalm 86:11) To love and serve the Lord Jesus Christ is to live daily facing this contrast between the world, and the life we are called to live in Jesus. He, alone, can help us meet this challenge as we seek Him in prayer, and yield to His guiding hand in the circumstances of life.

BIBLE KNOWLEDGE

My wife and I usually watch the quiz show Jeopardy. One evening was a teen challenge night. The three contestants were exceptionally sharp kids. They knew the answers to questions on a wide variety of subjects. They tried to beat each other to be the first one to answer the question. Sometimes Biblical questions come up. That evening one question asked, "What are the first five words of the 23rd Psalm in the King James version of the Bible?" Now that is probably the best know of all passages in the Old Testament. "The Lord is my Shepherd" Not one of the young people even attempted an answer. I find this incredible sad. And it is not uncommon. Most contestants regardless of age usually shy away from Biblical questions. We have become a people learned in all fields of human knowledge, yet ignorant in the one field that really matters. We are smart people without the true wisdom to know what to do with the learning we have. Sad, incredible sad, and it will ultimately lead to our downfall.

A Face Set Like Flint

As Jesus headed south from Galilee for the last time it says in one passage that His face was set to go to Jerusalem.^(Luke 9:51KJV) Jesus had one task to fulfill and he would not be deterred. His face was set. He had told the disciples what was going to happen and they couldn't understand it. He said that He must suffer, be crucified, and be raised on the third day. They didn't believe that this could possibly be God's plan for their Lord. He was doing too much good for the people, and they were sure He would fulfill the prophecies about returning the kingdom to Israel. As we go through this Lenten Season we move in a steady progression through these seven weeks to the events of Holy Thursday and Good Friday. Our faces are set in this one direction toward the cross. It is that, and that alone, that means our cleansing from sin and our ability to stand before Almighty God cleansed and holy in the righteousness of Jesus Christ. Like those first followers we would like to get around this. We don't want to be reminded of our desperate need for cleansing from our sinful nature. But there is no other way. It is when we set our faces towards the cross that we can rightly and fully celebrate the glorious resurrection on Easter Sunday morning.

Looking Into The Depth

When I look at a computer screen with its words, figures, and colors, the patterns communicate something to me. The information is to be useful and informative. But what I see is only the surface of the machine. What makes it work, forming all the outward patterns that convey information, is a complex series of electronic circuits and impulses hidden deep within the computer. The same is true for people. What people see in us is only the outward words, mannerisms, and actions we display. But those words, mannerisms, and actions are generated deep within our being, by the thought, attitudes, and convictions we hold. As Christians those thoughts and convictions are to be guided by God's Word, and our relationship with our Saviour. It is He who changes us from the inside, working in our hearts by the presences of His Spirit. Then, what others see is something of the love and nature of Jesus. As we concentrate on what forms our inward parts, the outward will follow naturally.

SETTING ASIDE OUR "I WANTS"

Getting children to do something isn't always easy. Parents will call them to come and they will continue to watch TV or stay at the game they are playing. A second, third, even fourth call will come, usually with increasing volume. God's people are often like that. The "I wants" are always strong in us. Like children wanting to continue our game we ignore the voice of our Lord. This is stated numerous time in the Old Testament. Shortly before their captivity and the destruction of Jerusalem, God said through Jeremiah, "These wicked people, who refuse to listen to my words, who follow the stubbornness of their hearts..."(Jeremiah 13:10) Relating to God is not so much a matter of following some set of dos and don'ts, but listening to His voice. He has spoken to us clearly in both Testaments of Scripture. His words are that of a Father who has done all for our good. In listening to His word we learn to know Him, to want to be a part of Him, and to willing yield more of our "I wants" for His direction in life.

God Is In Everyday Life!

Do we marginalize God? I ran across that phrase recently in an article I read, and I think it rings true. Surveys have shown that the majority of people believe in God, but they don't see God very much involved in every day life. Also the general concept of God is anything but the true God of the Bible. Even further if God seems to conflict with what we believe is right or want to do He is set aside or rationalized away. Almighty God is the one who created us. He made us for His good purpose establishing a pattern of life that was for our best Good. We rebelled (and continue to do so) from Him, yet He refused to give up of us. In love He gave His only begotten Son to provide our redemption. His Spirit is active in and around us even if we are not aware of Him. He created us. He redeemed us. He is actively working for us. We may close our hearts to Him, but He is a God who cannot be left in the margins of life.

A FEARFUL WORLD

We live in a very fearful world. We face illness, disease, natural disasters, financial stresses, environmental concerns, the evils that men do to one another, and more. The news media brings us a constant flow of bad reports. We feel relatively safe within our homes and communities, but keep a caution eye out for trouble. The biblical world was equally uncertain for the course of a human life. Yet it was to that world, and ours, that Scripture speaks. God spoke through Isaiah, "Do not fear, for I am with you; do not be dismayed, for I am your God. I will strengthen you and help you; I will uphold you with my righteous right hand."(Isaiah 41:10) Jesus, Almighty God incarnate, came among us to share this fearful life, and to break the power of death for all time. He taught us of God's Kingdom, a realm beyond fear, a realm that we share even now through faith in Him. We will still face many fearful things throughout our years, but in Jesus Christ we know that those things are not the final word. In Him we have strength to endure. Paul encourages us saying, "Do not be anxious about anything, but in every situation, by prayer and petition, with thanksgiving, present your requests to God. And the peace of God, which transcends all understanding, will guard your hearts and your minds in Christ Jesus."(Philippians 4:6-7)

Are We Different?

When we consider God's call to Noah, to Abraham, and to Moses we see that in each case they were called to come out of a pagan culture. They were to listen and be obedient to God, and then lead their people into a different way of life. We could also look at the whole nation of Israel, for that was their calling as well. In fact, that is the definition of what Christ's church is to be - people called out to live a different life in obedience to our Lord. It is not that we are better than anyone else. We are all sinful by nature, but we have been shown a better way of life in harmony with God. The problem with the church today is that, by many measures, it is not distinguishable from the surrounding culture. The walk of each of the Old Testament figures, and in fact for all of us, begins with hearing the call of our Lord to come and follow Him. He has given us His Holy Word both as a declaration of His redeeming love and as a guide in living a life pleasing to Him. It is that life that is to be a witness to the world and draw others to Him.

Don't Be Self Conscious About Praying

Don't be afraid to pray! Well that seems like a strange statement. We all pray when we are in need or have a care for someone. But I am thinking about praying for someone on the spot when a need is expressed. You don't need a pastor as the "official pray-er". I have found in many situations that more will happen in a few minutes of prayer than in many minutes of conversation. I've prayed with my neighbor when he was sitting on his lawn tractor and really hurting from a bad relationship. I've prayed with neighbors on both sides for things they were going through. But I'm a pastor, that's what I'm supposed to do. No! I'm a Christian, as you are, and that's what we are supposed to do. We hesitate because we feel self conscious. We are not sure of the right words, or what the person will think. None of that really matters if it seems that, in a given situation, the Holy Spirit is prompting us to pray. God can give us the words. God even takes our halting expressions and uses them for good. It is simply our hearts reaching out in Christ's love for the good of another. So, I say again. Don't be afraid to pray.

GOD DOES GOD TO US

The emphasis at one of our Pastor's Conference was on the need for each pastor to take time for quiet and spending time with the Lord Jesus. In numerous place Scripture speaks of learning to be quiet and waiting upon the Lord. Being still and letting the Lord renew one's strength. An interesting statement came up in one of our discussions that I offer to you to ponder, and hopefully take to heart. In our times of prayer, "God does God to me". It sounds a bit strange but think about it. From the beginning of creation God has desired to draw us into a deep and abiding relationship with Himself. Sin has broken that relationship, but in His grace God gave the redeeming blood of His Son, Jesus Christ, to make it possible for that relationship to be restored. For those who come to Him in humble, child like faith He comes drawing them into His perfect life. This is also spoken of a number of time as "entering into His rest". So when one comes in the quietness of their heart "God does God to them". Ponder this a bit. There is something very beautiful and powerful here.

It's In Genesis

All of the essential truths of life have their foundation in the book of Genesis, and particularly the first three chapters. God is our creator. We were made by Him and for Him. He made us in His image, reflected in the two genders of male and female. Imagery in both the Old and New Testaments likens our relationship to the Lord as that of the marriage relationship established in Genesis where the two become one. We also see the sin that entered the hearts of mankind when our first parents chose to lift their will above God's will. They found themselves naked and estranged from the love of their Creator bringing great burdens upon what had been a perfect and beautiful life. We see the consequences of that first sin displayed in newspapers and broadcasts daily. The third chapter ends with a prophetic image of the sacrifice of Christ. God graciously provides a blood sacrifice of one of His own creatures to replace the ill conceived fig leaves covering their nakedness with skins of flesh. For apart from God's gracious sacrifice, ultimately of His own Son, Jesus Christ, there could be no cleansing from sin. Don't get caught up in the creation/evolution debate and miss the clear truth He has provided in His Word.

SEEK THE LORD

Psalm 105 begins with words of praise for the Lord, then goes on in verses 3 and 4 saying "Let the heart of those who seek the LORD be glad. Seek the LORD and His strength; Seek His face continually." It is striking how often Scriptures encourages us to seek the Lord. Moses wrote to his people as they were about to enter Canaan. "But from there you will seek the LORD your God, and you will find Him if you search for Him with all your heart and all your soul."(Deuteronomy 4:29) And many years later from the Prophet Isaiah, "Seek the LORD while He may be found; Call upon Him while He is near. Let the wicked forsake his way And the unrighteous man his thoughts; And let him return to the LORD, And He will have compassion on him, And to our God, For He will abundantly pardon."(Isaiah 55:6-7) The Lord knows where we are. He knows us to the depth of our hearts. He is never far off and cares about all that touches us. Yet we do not know Him as we should. He has been perfectly revealed to us in His Son Jesus Christ, but it takes time in the Scriptures, in prayer, and in meditation to know Him. He wants us to know Him and to draw near to Him. Make it your aim in life to know the Lord who loves you with the deepest of love.

WHERE IS THE BLAME?

Since I took a look at the Psalms yesterday I'll continue today with the next one, number 106. The Psalms are very human expressions of both the good and the bad in people. Psalm 106 has a series of lessons about how God cared for His people, Israel, and how they soon forgot His care and rebelled from Him. I think of that today as some people will see the flooding that wipes out homes and livelihoods, tornadoes that destroy whole towns, senseless killings that take too many lives, and they ask the question "how could a good God of love allow these things? He's not a god I want to believe in." But those same people seem to forget the years of providence, of blessings, and of good that God has given. They seem to think that the good is somehow of their own intelligence and ability, while the bad is blamed on God. On the contrary, the fault is all ours. We are sinful and rebellious people to the core. It is this that has broken our world. Any good that exists is purely of God's grace, and the greatest of that grace is seen in the redeeming sacrifice of His Son, Jesus Christ. It is only in the light of that grace that we can understand anything in our broken world. Let's not be those who forget.

PSALM 118 FOR TODAY

"This is the day which the LORD has made; Let us rejoice and be glad in it."[(Psalm 118:24)] I don't know what you have planned for today, or whether you circumstances are good or bad. Even so this verse sets the tone for our days. Whether good or bad we are assured that the Lord is not far off. He is a part of our days with wisdom, guidance, strength, and help. This Psalm is also part of the messianic psalms. Just two verses before this one is the verse Jesus applied to Himself when talking to the Jewish leaders. "The stone which the builders rejected Has become the chief corner stone." Jesus is our Chief Corner Stone in all times and in all situations. He is the Rock on which we stand and in whom we have hope. You may want to take time to read all of Psalm 118. It is certainly a good one for each day.

Embedded In Us

Paul wrote in Romans 1 that what can be known about God is clearly seen in the things God has made. Scripture is clear in declaring that mankind is the intentional creation of our gracious Lord. As we understand from the early chapters of Genesis we were made pure and without sin, but we rebelled from that state, seeking our own will rather than God's will. However, there are several things that remain imbedded is all humans. We all have a desire for peace, security, well-being, and a good relationship with others. Further, as God gave His laws for the good of mankind, the basics of the Ten Commandments - to honor parents, not to steal, murder, commit adultery, to lie - are also imbedded in us, and are found universally the world over. We may deny this. We may harden our hearts and deaden our consciences, but they are still there. We live in much confusion caused by sin, but there is a basic desire to return to the Garden from which we were expelled. God has barred the way to Eden, but He has provided the way for our ultimate return. That path leads through the cross on Calvary's hill.

Blessings Abound

Holy Lord you have given your church many men and women of faith who have written hymns to praise you and to strengthen our lives for each day. One of those has left us with the assurance that you give "strength for today and great hope for tomorrow". Lord, how we need this assurance. Some of what we have to do today is the routine part of living, but other tasks are difficult or even hurtful. We don't have all wisdom, but you do. We don't have the strength sufficient for every task, but you do. Thank you for the promise never to leave or forsake us, and for the assurance that whatever we face today that is not the final word. There is hope for tomorrow. That same hymn writer followed this great promise by saying "blessings abound and ten thousand beside". We have seen your hand of blessing in our lives in many ways over all of our past years. We can only bow in humble worship giving glory to your holy name. Through Jesus Christ our Savior and Lord. Amen.

A Treasure in Our Hymnody

The prayer I prayed in yesterday's message was based on the hymn Great Is Thy Faithfulness. The hymnody that has been given to the Church over the past centuries is a great treasure, and a source of inspiration for our prayers. One that I use frequently in prayer was written in 1744 by a Welsh Christian named William Williams. "Guide me, O thou great Jehovah, pilgrim through this barren land. I am weak, but thou art mighty; Hold me with thy powerful hand. Bread of heaven, bread of heaven, Feed me till I want no more. Feed me till I want no more." Some of the praise choruses we sing in church are good, and I love many of the old Gospel songs, but don't neglect the hymnody of the church which has been passed down to us by devout Christian men and women through many centuries of our faith. Hymn lyrics can reinforce good theological teachings about our Lord, about the Holy Trinity, the truth of the Gospel, and more. They can aid us with words of praise drawing us closer to our Lord. "Praise to the Lord the Almighty the king of creation. O my soul praise him for his is thy health and salvation." These words written centuries ago become our own. They focus our attention on Him to whom all of our love and devotion is due. Let this great treasure of Christian thought draw you nearer to Him.

Male and Female, Christ and the Church

In a previous message I said that we were created in God's image, and that that image is reflected in the two genders of male and female. Further, I said that both Old and New Testaments likens our relationship with God to that of a marriage where the two become one. It is in this becoming one that we have the basis for our salvation. Five hundred years ago Martin Luther wrote, "For, if he (Christ) is a husband, he must take to himself that which is his wife's (us, the Church), and, at the same time, impart to his wife that which is his. For, in giving her his own body and himself, how can he but give her all that is his?(righteousness) And, in taking to himself the body of his wife, how can he but take to himself all that is hers?(our sins)" Our salvation has its truth in the fact that at the cross Jesus took all of our sins into Himself, and graciously gave us His righteousness. In the understanding of our relationship with the Lord as that of a marriage of husband and wife, male and female in a covenant for life, we see the magnificent nature of the grace of salvation God has provided. If we seek to modify this image of the marriage covenant, and of gender itself, as much of society is doing today we confuse and misunderstand the very basis of our salvation in Christ

One Nation Under God?

In a case before the Supreme Court a while back the court ruled that it is acceptable to open government meetings with prayer. Opponents, along with the dissenting judges, see prayer as an establishment of religion by the government. For them it is no longer a matter of insuring that we allow all faiths to participate. We already have that. Opponents want no recognition of any god at all. This is where we have come in a country founded by men, all of whom believed in God. They all believed in natural law established by God and binding on all people. I do not claim that all of our founders were Christian, they were not. But they all acknowledged God's existence, and the need to follow and appeal to Him for guidance and grace on our nation. Our modern times show us the pressure we are under to deny, or water down the practice of our faith, and challenges us to stand firm in what we believe. The U.S. Supreme Court has not and will not end all of the challenges to our faith. It is up to us to know what we believe, and be willing to stand firm on that belief.

Part of the Maker in What He makes

I have mentioned before about being a woodworker. I have learned a lot about life and about our Lord through this craft. Over the years I have made a lot of different pieces of furniture and cabinetry. A number of those pieces are in my house. One thing I realize is that there is something of me in each of the pieces. I know the steps each piece took in order to be completed, and the ease or difficulty of those steps. I know the hours invested and the thought required. If a piece would not be used or treated properly I would feel bad about it. So what has all this to do with our Lord. There is a verse in Luke 13:34 where Jesus laments, "O Jerusalem, Jerusalem, the city that kills the prophets and stones those sent to her! How often I wanted to gather your children together, just as a hen gathers her brood under her wings, and you would not have it!" Think about that. God made us in the beginning, male and female, together reflecting His image, who He is. Think about the investment God has in us, something of Himself in our being. When we sin we sully that image. We misuse our bodies, minds, and spirits in ways God never desired for His intended good and our intended blessing. We hurt God, our Maker, causing Him to lament even as Jesus did in the above verse. We take seriously who God is and who we are before Him. Don't take this lightly. This is the deeply serious nature of our life. We bow before Him trusting in the grace His has so wonderfully provided in His Son, Jesus, our Saviour.

A Christian

Many people claim to be Christian, and we will refer to people in the past, particularly our Founders, as being Christian, but is that really true? We always need to be clear in what we mean by being Christian. A follower of Jesus Christ is not a sufficient definition. That may simply mean that they like some of His teachings, and follow His moral precepts. The Apostle Paul wrote more clearly that, "If you declare with your mouth, 'Jesus is Lord,' and believe in your heart that God raised him from the dead, you will be saved."(Romans 10:9) A Christian is one who knows their eternal salvation rests only in the one man who has broken the power of death for all time, and declares Him to be Lord of their life. It is only in this that we stand justified before God, and have the assurance of our eternal life with Him. It is in this that the great truth of the Gospel, the Good News of Jesus Christ rests. It is in this that we have cleansing from sin and freedom from guilt. A Christian knows that Jesus is no mere moral teacher among all the rest, but the unique and only Saviour of mankind.

O Sacred Head Now Wounded

At our Wednesday evening Lenten service we sang the hymn O Sacred Head Now Wounded. It is an important penitential hymn going back to the 12th century. It's second verse particularly struck me. "How art thou pale with anguish, With sore abused and scorn; How does that visage languish Which once was bright as morn! Thy grief and bitter passion We're all for sinners gain; Mine, mine was the transgression, but thine the deadly pain." It give a clear picture of our Lord hanging on the cross. We've heard or read medical descriptions of the horrible suffering that crucifixion causes. That was God hanging on that cross! That was God bearing the punishment our sins deserve. That was God suffering the agony of total separation from the Father, the hell our rebellion rightly deserves. "Mine, mine was the transgression, but thine the deadly pain." Why did Jesus do it? Out of pure and absolute love for you, and for me. It was the pure grace of God that did this for us which we are incapable of dong for ourselves. In Jesus alone we can stand cleansed and free in God's presence. In Jesus alone we have life. Our only possible response is humble worship

God Created Us Complete and Without Sin

I have emphasized often that God is the author and source of life. People debate Scripture's truth about our creation versus evolution with its emphasis on billions of years of the cosmos existence. That doesn't concern me all that much. I don't know what happened to this 8000 mile diameter ball of rock we live on before God said, "let there be light" bringing order out of chaos. What I do express as an essential truth of our faith is that we did not come from some lower form of life, and that at some point in time past, we were created by God, complete and without sin. And further, it was from this sinless initial state that we later rebelled from the will of our God, becoming estranged from Him ever since. If it were not true that we began in a sinless relationship with our Creator, and later broke that relationship by our rebellion, there would be no need for a Redeemer, and the whole of Scripture becomes reduced to ancient history topped off with a few moral lessons. This, tragically, is the way many treat God's Word today. The message we declare in Jesus Christ is that, apart from Him, we are eternally separated from our Creator. By His gracious sacrificial act we have been redeemed and restored to our Lord.

What Do You Know For Sure?

A friend once asked me an unusual question. "What do you know for sure?" How would you answer that? What is it that you know for certain? I really don't know what the rest of this day will hold, or tomorrow, even with the plans I've made. As much as I try to take care of myself I don't know if my health will hold up. I don't know what the national economy will do, and I can't be 100% sure that my own economy will last through my life. I expect you can go through your own list of unknowns. So what can we say we know for certain? My response to my friends question - "That I am loved." Of that I am totally certain. I don't doubt or question that I am loved by my wife and family. It is a very solid rock for me. And above all I am certain of the love my Lord has for me. I don't understand a lot of things. Most of life is uncertain. But God has demonstrated His love for me, that even while I am still a sinful being, Christ died for me.(Romans 5:8) I hope you can respond in the same way. Hold to it. You are loved. Let that be your rock, your anchor, for this day and every day.

God Is Presence In All Of Our Days

What is on your schedule for today? Maybe a series of routine tasks for work or home. Maybe more serious items that have caused worry and fear. Either way they are things we must face and deal with as best we can. But in the grace of our Lord God we know that we face nothing alone. That really is the point of yesterday's message emphasizing that we are loved. God is with us. In the praise of our God Psalm 68 declares "Blessed be the Lord, who daily bears our burden, The God who is our salvation. God is to us a God of deliverance; And to GOD the Lord belong escapes from death." (vss.19-20) As any father knows they are never really separated from their children. What concerns the children concerns the father. God is our Father, and has more care for us than any earthly father. Our burdens are on His heart, and He is able to help. Whatever this day holds, whether routine or difficult, know that you are love and that the Lord is with you. Trust Him.

HOUSES BUILT ON SAND

I have used this Psalmist question before. He asked, "If the foundations are destroyed, What can the righteous do?"[(Ps.11:3)] But it is becoming more and more relevant. There was an article in the paper this week about a number of libraries around the country having a Drag Queen Story Hour for kindergartners and young children. A drag queen, as you probably know, is a man rather outlandishly dressed as a women. There have been other reports of teaching materials in the early school grade about a child having two mommies, or two daddies, normalizing the gay lifestyle. Now I've said before that I'm not against anyone, and that all people deserve to be treated with compassion and respect. But that doesn't mean we normalize their behavior. By educating our youngest children in these practices we are destroying the foundation of life as God intended it to be - and to be for our best good. But we've already seen many more years where the Bible has been ignored. It is the most sold and least read book in the world. We have no foundation in God's Holy Word so why should we not do these other things. "What can the righteous do?" We can pray. Pray for guidance and wisdom. We can pray for the Lord to shorten the time to His return. We can read God's Word, and hold fast to its truth, even if that is personally costly. We can show the love of Christ to all people praying that we draw some into that love. Satan is working hard to destroy our foundations, but he will not win. The love of Christ displayed at the cross defeated the power of sin and death. It will continue to do so through us.

Patience and Persistence

I like walnuts, but did you ever see the walnut just off of the tree? It is a large, hard green pod. The pod must be broken open. Inside is a black sticky goo that stains everything in sight. Only then, when that is all cleaned off, do you get to the shell, which then has to be carefully cracked to get to the nut. A lot of time, patience, and persistence is involved in getting to the meat. Here we have another analogy to our faith. Scripture, time and again, invites us to invest the time, seeking God with patience and persistence. The world, the flesh, and the devil is the goo that distracts us with many "important things" that need to be taken care of first, as well as very busy schedules. It takes persistence, and we fail, but we keep at it. We will find that the meet of the Word is really good food. Jeremiah 29:13 says, "you will seek me and find Me when you seek Me with all of your heart." Knowing and walking with our Lord should be the deepest desire of our hearts.

THE RIGHT PATH

Following is an important task for a Christian. But it is important to carefully determine who we follow. Around Washington one is supposed to follow the politically correct path, and maintain the image of power. In academic circles one must write and teach according to the accepted social and scientific standards. Even in grade school children want to follow the current fashions and trends. Society dislikes one who is different since it is perceived as saying society is wrong. But it was Jesus who said, "If anyone would come after me, he must deny himself and take up his cross and follow me." [Matthew 16:24] Jesus continually lived in a way different from the society around Him. In the deepest love He sought to show that God had a better way of life for all people. He invites us to follow Him, knowing that if we do we, too, will face opposition. Following what the world dictates may lead to some worldly success and honors, but following Jesus leads to life.

FOR ALL SEASONS

In the Lenten Season we focus on the atoning sacrifice our Lord made on our behalf. Not that this great act of grace can ever be confined to one season, but the penitential aspect of this time brings the cross very personally home to each one of us. There is a wonderful hymn for this time from the prolific 18th century hymn writer Isaac Watts. Its first two verses say, "Alas! and did my Savior bleed, And did my Sovereign die? Would he devote that sacred Head for sinners such as I? Was it for sin that I had done He groaned upon the tree? Amazing pity, grace unknown, and love beyond degree." In these words the sacrifice of our Lord becomes very personal. We can't get away by saying "I'm not so bad." We all fall short of the Glory of God which is our standard for life.[Romans 3:23] This gracious act of Christ on Calvary was done "for me" … "for you". That sacrifice alone is the source of our lives. Apart from it we are lost in our sin. "But drops of grief can ne'er repay the debt of love I owe. Here, Lord, I give myself to away; tis all that I can do."[vs.5]

Not That He Couldn't - But He Wouldn't!

When Jesus was hanging on the cross on that dark Friday one of the taunts bystanders threw at Him was "He saves others, He cannot save Himself". They meant as mocking, but they were speaking the truth. He couldn't save Himself. After pleading for another way, He had yielded Himself to His Father's will in the Garden of Gethsemane. He was fulfilling the plan that had been put in place before creation. All of God's prophets had spoken of this time, and their words must prevail. No, He couldn't save Himself. If He could God's plan for the redemption of mankind would not have been completed. You and I would still be in our sins and with no hope for eternal life with God. What people were witnessing on that Friday, and unknowingly testifying to with their mocking, was the greatest act of salvation the world has ever known. It was the most perfect act of love and grace. We humbly bow in adoration to the Lord who couldn't save Himself.

PASSION

Passion is an interesting word. It is usually associated with strong romantic or sexual feelings. The dictionary defines it as strong feelings of enthusiasm or excitement for something or about doing something. The time of our Lord's suffering from the Last Supper to His crucifixion is called The Passion. Our Lord had the deepest love for mankind, and commitment to He Heavenly Father that set His course to willingly suffer, making atonement for all of our sins. Another word is zeal. Which is fervor for a person, cause or object. God is spoken of as having zeal for His people, and a number of individuals in Scripture are referred to as having zeal for the Lord. It is that strong feeling, that fervor, that has driven people throughout the Christian centuries to sacrifice their own time and well being for the good of others, and even to hold their convictions to the point of a martyr's death. It is the knowledge that we are loved with the everlasting love of God that we are willing to do everything necessary to remain in and share that love.

Easter is This Week, Too!

We had a great worship service yesterday celebrating our Lord's resurrection. Church was full. We sang great hymns, heard a fine message, gathered around the altar to share the Holy Sacrament, and declared again He is Risen! He is Risen Indeed! But today Monday. We have a week before us of routine work, some pleasant tasks, some not so pleasant. The week may contain some illness, or a funeral service, as ours did last week. So as great as our service was yesterday, we are back in the midst of life today. But that is just the point of all that yesterday's service proclaimed. Our Lord knows who we are and all we face in day to day life in a broken world. God sent His only begotten Son into this world to bring us life, not just for one special day but for every day. "I have come", Jesus said, "that you may have life, and have it to the full."(John 10:10) In the resurrection of Jesus Christ from the grave the power of sin, death, and the devil have been broken. Through faith in His name we have life. Today is Monday. The Lord is Risen! He is Risen Indeed!

Measure Him or Trust Him?

How do we measure God? That may seem like a strange question, but I think we have the tendency to measure God all the time. For example, Is God good only when He gives us what we think are good things? That seems to the thought behind statements like - How could a good God......? or If God is a God of love why .....? This is god made in our image, which is something we try too often to do. God Himselfdeclares, "For my thoughts are not your thoughts, neither are your ways my ways. As the heavens are higher than the earth, so are my ways higher than your ways and my thoughts than your thoughts."(Isaiah 55:8-9) Many of God's ways are hidden to us, but He has revealed Himself throughout Scripture as the Creator God who loves and works for the good of His creation. Rather than try to measure God by our standards, we do well to come in humble trust to Him who has shed the blood of His own Son for our redemption.

BEING PREPARED

This has been a mild winter here on the central U.S. coast. We've had not much more than two inches of snow all totaled - for which I'm quite happy. But it's always interesting what happens when a snowy weather forecast comes out. People head for the grocery stores in a rush to be prepared. We've got have our milk. bread , and toilet paper. Jesus once observed this same response with the leaders of His day. "You know how to interpret the appearance of the sky," He said, "but you cannot interpret the signs of the times."(Matthew 16:3) With all of our technology, we do a marvelous job (sometimes) predicting the weather. We prepare for what is coming by wearing the right clothes, taking an umbrella, picking up extra items, whatever is needed. Yet we fail in the one area that is important above all, understanding the times we live in. In these times mankind has grown far from the purpose for which God created us. Both Old and New Testaments speak of the time when Christ would return to earth. Jesus taught us that we should watch, and be prepared. This is not by building shelters and stockpiling food, but preparing our hearts. He is looking for hearts that are set on Him in love, and longing for His presence. We are to live each day by faith in the Lord Jesus Christ, in a deep desire to have Him physically present, and, while we are consciously waiting, in showing His love through our actions to others. That is our greatest preparation, and today really could be the day.

SEEING THE RESULTS

They say that seeing is believing. We like to see the results of the things we hold to be true. When we flip a light switch, we don't see the electron running through the wires inside the wall, but we see the light come on, so we believe that the electrons are there. Just because we don't see a result doesn't mean that something isn't happening. A light bulb may be burned out, but the electrons are still in the wire. So it is with our prayers. We want to see the results of our prayers and often do, but there are times when we pray and pray with nothing seeming to happen. We always look at the outward results when our Lord begins His work on the inside. The Lord's greatest miracles are those of turning hearts to Him, of forgiving sins, of healing deep and long held hurts. These will be seen later on in changed lives, but there is so much happening that is unseen. It is why Jesus encourages us to continue to pray and not lose heart. He further said, "blessed are those who have not seen and yet believe." God does love you, care about you, and is working for your good far beyond anything your eyes presently see.

ONE THING I KNOW

Chapter nine of St. John's Gospel has the account of Jesus healing a man who was born blind. Of course He did it on the Sabbath which got him in trouble with the Pharisees. The Jewish leaders grilled the man who had been healed trying to get something they could use against Jesus. I really love this guy in the way he stood his ground against the officials. They tried to get him in a theological discussion which the man rejected. He simply said, "This one thing I know. Once I was blind, but now I can see." The Lord had worked in his life. He knew it, and he wouldn't back down. If you are a Christian, if you have known the Lord for some period of time, I think you can identify with this man. There is one, or perhaps a few, turing points in your life about which you can say, "This I know. Once I was blind, but now I see. I know the Lord worked in my life at that very point and I am changed because of it." You may not be able to explain it clearly to others so that it has the same meaning it has for you, but nonetheless it is real. Jesus touched you. For the healed blind man it led him to worship the Lord. Let it do the same for us.

COME INTO HIS WORLD, HIS LIFE

Jesus was always reversing things. He fulfilled perfectly the law God required of mankind, but He refused to be bound by the legality of the Pharisees. He called disciples to an important mission, but instead of great perks with the job He told them there would be suffering, persecution, and death. He offers us new life, the best life possible, but says that we must first die to ourselves and be reborn in Him. He submitted to governing authorities allowing them to murder Him so that He would become King of all kings and Lord of all lords. Following Christ means coming into His world, His life, His nature. And it is not always just the way we think it should be. Coming into a relationship with Jesus is not just matter of following some of the nice things we like Him. Jesus doesn't just offer us a nice moral standard to follow or an example how to love one another. He shows us the cross and says there alone you will find the life that really matters.

A Spiritual Battle

Just before the first murder where Cain killed his brother Abel, God had said to him "If you do what is right, will you not be accepted? But if you do not do what is right, sin is crouching at your door; it desires to have you, but you must master it."(Genesis 4:7) Jesus said, "Things that cause people to sin are bound to come.."(Luke 17:1) And even further Peter said, "Be self-controlled and alert. Your enemy the devil prowls around like a roaring lion looking for someone to devour. Resist him, standing firm in the faith..."(I Peter 5:8-9) We live in a fallen world with a myriad of enticements seeking to pull us away from the Lord, as well as the desires of our own flesh contrary to God's will. We have the total provision for forgiveness, healing, and new life in Jesus Christ, but we are admonished to "Put on the full armor of God so that you can take your stand against the devil's schemes."(Ephesians 6:11) We are in a spiritual battle in this world. We have more than ample provision in Christ to overcome sin, death, and the devil, but we must turn to Him and use the armor He has given, in order to "stand our ground, and after we have done everything, to stand."(Ephesians 6:13)

OUR HERITAGE

A couple months ago my wife and I had the fun of spending a long weekend with our daughter and son-in-law in the Boston area. The northeastern United States is a historic area. Much of the country's early settlement took place there 400 years ago. We visited the Plymouth Plantation, a recreated village site simulating the pilgrim's beginning in this country. We have known for a long time that my wife is an 11th generation decedent of the doctor who came over on the Mayflower. We took pictures of my wife and daughter (now 12th generation) standing in the doorway of that good doctor's crude 1621 one room cabin. Something to be proud of? Well, sure! It gives the family a solid tie to important events of the past. Though, in reading some of the literature a day or so later, there are now about 35,000,000 Mayflower descendants. Somehow that seems to take the edge off of any pride that might be involved. It will always be a valuable piece of family information, but even if there were only a few descendants there is still nothing one can hold up in pride. Whether little or much, whether new or quite old, whether seemingly good or bad, everything we have is a gift of God's grace. After all, Scripture says He knew us before we were born. We live day by day, neither in pride or self-contempt, but in great thanksgiving for the gifts (including our place in the world) God has chosen to bestow. We seek to use them for our continued growth, for the good of others, and to God's glory.

100 Continue Steadfast

We had the privilege of attending our grandson's confirmation at his church. Confirmation is that time when a young person has the opportunity to affirm the vows his parents took for him when he was baptized as an infant. It is a serious time, and for those in attendance it is an important reminder of the seriousness of our of own confession of the Christian faith. These young people had been instructed by their pastor for several years, and are then asked to stand before the congregation to confess their faith in the Lord Jesus Christ. After being asked a series of questions about their belief, they are asked one final question. "Do you intend to continue steadfast in this confession and church and to suffer all, even death, rather than fall away from it?" That becomes a question posed to all of us who profess faith in our Lord. It is especially true in an era where there have been more Christian martyrs than all previous centuries of the Church, and where even in our own country, people have been asked to compromise their faith In order to continue their business. So confirmation is not just a service our young people go through. It is a challenge for all of us to rethink the depth and commitment to our own faith. Our relationship with the Lord Jesus is truly worth what ever the cost.

The Power of Forgiveness

Forgiveness is a powerful and necessary characteristic for life. In our fallen state we all have our share of self-centeredness, and ignorance of others needs and feelings. This causes us to hurt and be hurt. It causes us to offend both God and others. The power to forgive and be forgiven was gained for us at the cross. It is vital that we depend upon daily. We have no life with God apart from the forgiveness granted us through Christ. We have no relationship with others unless we are willing to forgive, and to ask for forgiveness. Forgiveness has been given to us at the greatest possible cost. Let's be willing to use it in all of our relationships.

WE KNOW THE WAY

On Thursday evening shortly before Jesus' arrest and trial He was trying to comfort His disciple's fears. He had said to them, "You know the way to the place where I am going."(John 14:4) Then Thomas asked a question that summaries what all of us feel at times. "Lord, we don't know where you are going, so how can we know the way?" We believe in the Lord Jesus Christ. We are committed to Him. But we also live in a world that doesn't make a lot of sense, and we all face situations where we don't know the way. "Lord, where are you going with this? How can we know the right way?" Then Jesus answered,"I am the way and the truth and the life..." We would like to have a specific plan - do this, this, and this and all will work out well. That isn't the answer Jesus gives. He simply says keep your eyes on me, hold my hand, follow me. We don't know where many of our trials in life will end. Just like the disciples on that Thursday evening had no real ideal of all that they would face. Yet they walked forward keeping their eyes, and the deepest hope of their hearts fixed on Jesus. It was He who brought them through to the resurrection on Easter Sunday Morning. With eyes fixed on Jesus we move forward one step at a time.

24 Hour News Broadcasts

I read a book a while back entitled How The News Makes You Dumb. It's point was, given the necessity of filling 24 hours a day with some kind of material, there are redundant, and often conflicting reports that lead to more confusion than truth. News pages and air time are also filled with useless, and at times sensational details of people's lives that we really don't need to know. In the U.S. we have the constitutional guarantee of freedom of the press. This is a right to be cherished and guarded. But it also takes a great deal of discernment on our part to filter through what is useful and important, and what is not. This discernment, like everything else in a Christian's life, is guided by our understanding of God's Word, and His purpose for mankind. We view the world through God's truth, and the life we are called to in Jesus Christ. In this way we can skim over 80% of the news presented, and prayerfully take the remainder for whatever understanding or action is needed. I find it helpful to begin with the comics first!! That sets the rest in the proper perspective.

The Unexpected

We like to think that we are capable of doing what needs to be done, and for the most part we are. We have talents and abilities. We work by something of a routine. We solve many problems as they come along in our days. However, as smoothly as things go along for a while, something always seems to crop up reminding us that we are not always in control. Be it a computer glitch, a sudden illness that puts one in the hospital, or even an unexpected death, things happen that we can't change. The Lord, in His grace, uses these times to remind us to look beyond ourselves, check our priorities, set aside our pride, or a variety of other lessons aimed at focusing our attention upon Him for strength, wisdom, and guidance. No, we do not have the ultimate control of our lives. There is One far greater than we who does. And His nature is pure love and grace. Let's depend upon Him.

TALK ABOUT UNEXPECTED!

This has been an interesting and unexpected period of time for me since the first of the year. Starting with a hip replacement in January to open heart surgery May to repair a leaky mitral valve. All has gone well, but has left me with little energy, and an order to be patient and take it slow. These unexpected events will set the tone for a few Good Morning messages. My wife, Audrey, has done great in taking care of me. I still plan to continue writing my morning messages, and also figuring out what else is in the offing since my retirement in March. One thing I've tried to emphasize through all my messages is that our Gracious Lord is a part of <u>all</u> life, and there are things we can learn that draw us ever closer to our Saviour.

A Great and Varied Multitude

The University of Maryland Medical Center, where I currently reside for a few days until my heart valve issues are resolved, is a teaching hospital. It is a very large facility, multiple departments, and a staff that resembles the United Nations. The kind and competent nurses and technicians that have attended me come from many different nations and backgrounds. It reminds me of the verse in Revelation 7. "After these things I looked, and behold, a great multitude which no one could count, from every nation and all tribes and peoples and tongues, standing before the throne and before the Lamb, clothed in white robes, and palm branches were in their hands;"(7:9) I know nothing about the lives of these kind servants. They don't look like me and don't talk like me, but they give me a foretaste of that great company in heaven who will be my brothers and sisters in the faith. Look at any gathering of people and you see groups gathering in similar ethnic, racial, social and other clusters of similar individuals. According to John's vision heaven will be far more like what I am experiencing in this setting. There are many surprises awaiting us in God's Kingdom. This not the least of them.

FEARFULLY AND WONDERFULLY MADE

There things to be learned all around us. I find that there are a number of lessons being reinforced by my hospital stay. One I see all around me in this place. This is a large teaching hospital. There are whole departments, even buildings dedicated to just one part of the human body. Every staff member testifies to the complexity and the marvel of the human body. I certainly see this with all that has been explained to me about just one valve of my heart. Incredible! David knew the truth of this thousands of years ago when he wrote: "For You formed my inward parts; You wove me in my mother's womb. I will give thanks to You, for I am fearfully and wonderfully made;..." (Psalm 139:13-14) We are too complex to be the product of chance. You were made, I was made, by God and for God. Sin has tainted our bodies, but they are a marvel of God handiwork none the less. And the skill God has given to those who attend us is no less amazing. The more we see of what God has done the more we are brought to our knees in worship.

Spiritual Heart Surgery

When you read this I will likely be in the hospital ICU, or perhaps back in my room after the heart valve operation. Think about what has been happening to me in these last couple of days. One cannot live without their heart pumping the life giving blood throughout the body. It is bringing oxygen to every cell. When the heart is defective in any way the entire body cannot function to its capacity. We know this so clearly with our physical bodies, but there is a more important spiritual counterpart. We were created by God to be in fellowship with Him. He gave us a spiritual heart to make that fellowship possible. But sin has corrupted that heart just the same as whatever malady caused my bad heart valve. Yet far more serious even than the physical! It is a malady that separates us from our Lord, and very truly leads to spiritual death. We need a spiritual heart operation, and that is just what Jesus did. His death on Calvary was not an unfortunate set of circumstances. It was the intentional provision of our Gracious God. It is the only provision for our spiritual life-giving heart surgery. We do everything possible for our physical wellbeing as testified by the massive hospital complex I am now in. How much more should we do everything possible for our eternal spiritual wellbeing. In Jesus is life, and His life is the Light of men. (John 1:4)

ALL IN RIGHT ORDER

I've said there are many lessons to learn about life from the workings of the human body. Paul had written that what can be know about God is clearly seen in the things God has made. One of the most complex of those things is the body. I'm learning more here in the hospital about the importance of balance. They are giving me numerous pills and injections, but they have to draw blood samples to test that all things stay in balance. One medication does what it is supposed to do without throwing other things off. (All in layman's terms of course.) But isn't that what God has been telling us all along with the life He created for us to live. Scripture give us the way of life that is for our good. To ignore that is called sin, but more importantly is separates us from our God who love us deeply, and has shown us the way that we will have the best and most joyful life possible. When we do things in the physical body that support life we find health and activity. If not, we find illness. When we follow those things God has given for our spiritual well- being we find wholeness and joy. If not, we find spiritual illness. This is not some legal demand to follow a set of statutes. It is simply understanding who God is and why He made us, and wanting to come more deeply into His life.

DON'T FORGET YOUR SPIRITUAL EXERCISE

We continually hear the benefits of diet and exercise being voiced. We are told that for good physical health a regular exercise routine is important. This is especially true where I presently reside. I think we all understand this, whether or not we are disciplined enough to follow through. However, there are other types of exercise that are equally, and actually more, essential. We must continue to exercise our minds through reading, studying something new, various mental games, being aware of current events, and so forth. Our minds at every age continue to need stimulation. Then there is also, I believe the most important and oft neglected, spiritual exercise. Time for Scripture and worship, both private and public, pondering the truths of our Lord, learning to be quiet in spirit allowing the Holy Spirit to speak. It is spiritual exercise that gives meaning and direction to all the rest. It is this exercise that gives joy to life in a deepening fellowship with God eternal. It is spiritual exercise that makes us alive to God, and of service to others. Paul wrote to his spiritual son Timothy, "On the other hand, discipline yourself for the purpose of godliness; for bodily discipline is only of little profit, but godliness is profitable for all things, since it holds promise for the present life and also for the life to come." (I Timothy 4:7-8)

Is God Too Slow?

In our hurry up world we want to see everything accomplished yesterday. Computers do computations at speeds of gigahertz per second, but this often feel too slow in getting the information we want. In our Christian life we would like to see things happening faster. We get frustrated if we don't see answers to our prayers when we hoped. Changes in our own lives don't seem to happen quickly enough. I think we have learned from Scripture and from life that God doesn't work in our time frame. He works according to His divine purpose for each of us, and like any project, must do things in the proper order. Peter wrote in his epistle, "The Lord is not slow in keeping his promise, as some understand slowness. He is patient with you, not wanting anyone to perish, but everyone to come to repentance." (2 Peter3:9) Sometimes God acts sovereignly for change. Most often He works step by step, His Spirit knowing what we need at the time, and dealing with first things first. He is always working for our good according to His perfect will. He asks us to trust Him, and give Him glory in all things.

I Do Believe! Help My Unbelief

There are times in the Gospels that Jesus seems to give us a blank check concerning our prayers. "Whatever you ask in My name, that will I do, so that the Father may be glorified in the Son."(John 14:13) Whatever you ask? But we know that there are things we ask in Jesus name and don't receive. Another time Jesus spoke about the power of faith and said, "All things you ask in prayer, believing, you will receive."(Matthew 21:22) Believing faith is a key, but that gives us a real problem. Doubts so easily assault us. When we pray for a healing and nothing happens, are we to blame for our lack of faith? I don't believe that is a burden of guilt the Lord intends us to bear. That kind of guilt can drive us to despair, and that's not where our Lord wants us. On another occasion a father came asking Jesus for healing for his son. Jesus asked if he believed He could do this. The father responded, "I do believe; help me overcome my unbelief!"(Mark 9:24) That is where our faith must rest - in the One who has the power to help us overcome. He is the One who has given His life to cleanse us from sin. He is the One who knows us to the depth of our hearts. We won't see all of our prayers answered just the way we ask, but we can trust ourselves into the hand of the One who loves us with an everlasting love.

Longing Too Be With The Beloved

Psalm 84 is a marvelous passage speaking about our hunger to be near the Lord. I remember the time when my wife and I were engaged. I was living with my parents. I would get home from work, have some supper, and then go over to Audrey's house. One time my mother remarked, "You don't have to go over every night." But I did. That is where I wanted to be. I was in love with her and wanted to be near her. That is the point of Psalm 84. "My soul yearns, even faints, for the courts of the LORD; ... O LORD Almighty, my King and my God. Blessed are those who dwell in your house; they are ever praising you. Better is one day in your courts than a thousand elsewhere;..." God is not a duty to be fulfilled. He is not a judge we need a appease with our good works. He is not a doctor who is the last resort in our troubles. God is our lover who has reached out to us before we ever thought of reaching out to Him. He is our redeemer demonstrating His love in the greatest of personal sacrifices. He is near at hand in good times and in bad. This is our God for whom our soul's yearn to draw ever nearer.

GOD GUIDES US IN HIS TRUTH

What is a catechism? For Christian churches a catechism is a basic series of statements that make up the core beliefs of our faith. We could refer to Luther's Small and Large Catechisms, the Westminster Catechism, and so forth. Christian Catechisms have their foundation in the Bible, the 66 books of the Old and New Testaments. We believe that the Bible is God's revealed word to mankind and therefore foundational for the things we hold to be true. They thus become the guide for the thoughts and actions of life. Recently an interviewer went to the Women's March in Washington, D.C. asking some basic questions about what a woman is, and what they were trying to say by their demonstration. What he found was a series of politically correct answers based on the climate of society in our day. That is a pretty shaky foundation that changes with the prevailing tone of the times. He referred to it as a modern catechism of beliefs that had been well learned by many, but that had a very changeable foundation. It is very hard to base one's life on such shifting sand. There are many questions that come up in the Christian life, and there are many doctrines stated in our catechisms. But we always have God's written word as our foundation to stand upon. We are supposed to question statements without blindly adopting them. But it is vitally important that we choose the right foundation upon which to stand. By God's grace through His Spirit He can guide us on the true path to His life.

WHAT IS REALLY NECESSARY?

It is interesting to observe the changes we've experienced over many years. We love our cell phones, smart phones, and iPads that keep us in touch with others wherever we are. If we are without it for a day we feel lost. It was only a few years ago that we would ride through a town looking for a corner phone booth if we needed to make a call. Show a young person a dial telephone and he'll wonder what it is. Many years ago people would go on a journey and be out of touch for months at a time. Our world has certainly changed. I'm not convinced it has all of been for good. How do we measure change? Or a deeper question, what is our purpose in life? According to the the Westminster Catechism, our purpose is to love God and enjoy Him forever. If that is true, then change is measured by how it supports this purpose, or perhaps detracts from it. People before mass communication learned to love God deeply and share His love with many others. We won't give up our cell phones, but we should keep our focus on the true purpose for which God has given us life.

Remembering Is Important

We set aside several days throughout the year to remember events in our national history. We set aside a day to remember those who serve in our armed service, and especially those who have given their lives to maintain our freedom. These are important to highlight the direction we have set, and the sacrifices necessary to maintain it. We also see this in Biblical times. The Jews set up a number of stone monuments at places of importance as they left slavery in Egypt. Fathers would tell their children what God did in those place for the good of His people. Christians have the cross as a constant reminder of the redeeming sacrifice our God has made on our behalf. We live near Washington, D.C. a place filled with monuments of our past. What is the point? It is covered by the simple phrase - lest they forget. Our history is important. The past actions of our Lord, and those of our ancestors, are important for understanding who we are. They give us direction and commitment for our present days. They remind us of the cost that has been paid for us to live life today, thus keeping us from being arrogant and self satisfied. Days of remembrance are important - lest we forget.

BUT WHAT IS INSIDE?

Reporters use adjectives to gain attention for their stories. The Comcast home page highlights top videos of the day, and usually of some prominent personality. When referring to women it will use words like "wows" or "stuns" referring to their dress, or lack thereof. So much of beauty today is sold on the basis of outward appearance. The media teaches girls, from their earliest ages, that their self worth is connected to their outward beauty. This is really very wrong, and something parents need to counteract. Scripture teaches us something quite different, saying to women that, "Your adornment must not be merely external--braiding the hair, and wearing gold jewelry, or putting on dresses; but let it be the hidden person of the heart, with the imperishable quality of a gentle and quiet spirit, which is precious in the sight of God." (I Peter 3:3-4) We all like to look nice when we go out, and that's fine. But that is not who we are. Those same news reports of beautiful celebrities often also show that they are not very nice people, or have messed up their lives in many ways. If we, men and women alike, learn to cultivate a heart that is deeply committed to Jesus, then a very special beauty can't help but be seen by others.

One Who Delights In The Lord

The Book of Psalms gives us wonderful expressions of lives lived in relationship to the Lord. Whether they are Psalms of praise, or cries for help, they address a Lord known to be near at hand and caring about individual concerns. They speak of a relationship where God is absolutely sovereign, where His will is to be sought and obeyed, yet recognizing that that path is the one leading to the best life for the Psalmists. The person "whose delight is in the law of the LORD, and who meditates on his law day and night. That person is like a tree planted by streams of water, which yields its fruit in season and whose leaf does not wither-- whatever they do prospers." (Ps.1:2-3) The Psalms speak of the affairs of individuals and of nations, of the God who made us and we are His. (Ps.100) Nations today are in such a rush to create secular societies, something that would have made no sense to the Psalmists. Fair treatment and justice are important in the Psalms, but never separated from a life lived with the Lord. "Righteousness and justice are the foundation of your throne; love and faithfulness go before you. Blessed are those who have learned to acclaim you, who walk in the light of your presence, LORD." (Ps.89:14-15) Yes, blessed are those who have learned to acclaim You.

TYPE A WITH A MEASURE OF HUMILITY

Do you remember the West Wing TV series of some years ago? West Wing was the drama series set in the White House. It followed the various high power characters through national and international situations. I once remarked that it was like putting 50 or so Type A personalities all in the same place, butting heads trying to solve problems. Now, Type A personalities are fine. They get a lot done and put their energy to good use. I think the Apostle Peter had such a personality. He was the first to move ahead, to seek a solution, to declare his allegiance, but he also needed to be tempered with humility, patience, and quieting of spirit. Sometimes a hard lesson to learn as it was with Peter when, after a great confession of allegiance, he denied the Lord three times. It took our Lord's redeeming grace on the shores of Galilee after His resurrection, to restore him. Only then was Peter truly useful in the Lord's service. The Psalmists has written, "Unless the LORD builds the house, They labor in vain who build it; ..." (Ps.127:1) We are not to be lazy or ignore problems that need to be dealt with, but this points out the necessity that all right directions need to be guided by the Lord. We can only hear His voice in humility and quietness of heart. Sometimes that means just sitting down, being quiet, and giving the Lord enough time to speak.

Pastor's Need To Stay Connected

One of our Pastor's Conference a few years ago emphasized the need for a pastor to have a strong devotional life. There were several presentations, but then a good bit of time was given for the men to separate, find a comfortable spot, and let the Lord minister to them. There was no planned agenda for that alone time. One could read Scripture, or a devotional book, take time for prayer, and if one fell asleep that was OK too. The point for these times was simply to allow Jesus to have access to our hearts. Simply being quiet in the Lord's presence. We are such a busy people with so many concerns this is a foreign concept. We are accomplishment driven, checking things off our "to do" lists. And they are all good things, but at times run ahead of the Lord in directions that accomplish less than if we had taken some quiet time in His presence. Israel's history is full of examples - think about their journey to the Promised Land. A journey that should have taken them six months took them forty years. Isaiah wrote, "the Holy One of Israel, has said, 'In repentance and rest you will be saved, In quietness and trust is your strength.'" Unfortunately they responded, "No, for we will flee on horses,..." (Isaiah 30:15-16) I think it was somewhat of a surprise to all of the pastors gathered at the Conference what actually did happen in those quiet hours.

The Beauty Around Us

I enjoy pictures of beautiful landscapes. Microsoft puts up a new landscape photo on my screen almost daily from various places around the world. There are so many around this globe. We have a hymn in our hymnal entitled For The Beauty Of The Earth which highlights all of the joy and beauty our Lord gives us in life. "For the beauty of the earth, for the beauty of the skies, for the love which from our birth over and around us lies..... for the joy of ear and eye, for the hearts and minds delight for the joy of human love, brother, sister, parent, child, friends on earth and friends above.... For thyself, best gift divine! To our race so freely given, for that great, great love of thine...." and each verse ends with, "Christ our God, to thee we raise this our sacrifice of praise." It is easy to see all that is wrong in our fallen world sometimes making it heard to see the beauty. But our God has not and will not abandon us. "For the beauty of each hour, of the day and of the night...." God provides us something to give hope, and helps us look ahead to all the joy and beauty He yet has for us. Lift up your eyes and see what our Lord provides for this day, and offer that "sacrifice of praise".

We Need To Praise God

Some years ago Merlin Carothers wrote a series of books on the power of praise. He showed how people who were willing to praise God even in the most difficult of circumstances saw great changes in their lives. There is much in Scripture about praising God. It is not that God is some egotistical being that need our praise, like the Romans and Greek gods fashioned in human images. It is we who need to praise God. Psalm 22, the great psalm depicting our Lord suffering on the cross, says "Yet You are holy, O You who are enthroned upon the praises of Israel."[(vs.3)], or as in the King James version translate it, "you inhabit the praise of Israel". In other words our praise bring us into the presence of our gracious God. By praising God we enter into His presence, and that changes things. Oh, we may still have to deal with difficult circumstances of life, but we know we are not alone. We are strengthened and supported by the Lord who is in control of all things. And in that we can find peace.

THE VALUE OF A GIFT

Everyone likes to get gifts, free stuff, huge discounts, or even win the lottery. But the thing we find with most such gifts is that they are short lived. Many gifts get put aside, free stuff is not all that useful, and many big lottery winners have found the money more of a curse than a blessing. The writer of the Book of James tells us that "Every good and perfect gift is from above, coming down from the Father of the heavenly lights, who does not change like shifting shadows." (James 1:17) We often seek after toys and baubles in life ignoring the One from whom our true treasure comes. It is the Lord who is the source of life. It is He who has given us life in Jesus Christ. God shows us in His Word the path to the best life possible. It is He who loves us with an everlasting love that never changes. Everything else we have in this world can be seen as a gift of God, and received with thankfulness and praise. Sure, getting gifts is nice, but we live daily in the joy of having already received the greatest gift possible, a relationship with Almighty God through faith in Jesus Christ. Everything else flows from this.

BASED ON THE EVIDENCE

When one goes to court evidence is presented concerning the case. Both sides try to convince the judge or jury of the truth of their position. Evidence is presented, witnesses brought forward, and all required to be the truth. The case is decided on the strength of the evidence on one side or the other. We believe in God, not out of some figment of imagination or wishful thinking, but because of evidence that has been established over generations, and confirmed in our own lives. We have the historic facts of God working with His people over thousands of years. We have the witness of those who have walked with Jesus Christ, testifying to His life, death, and resurrection. We have the truth of the Gospel enduring though 2000 years of Church history. We witness the touch of God's hand in all that He has created. Above all, we have the testimony confirmed in our own hearts. The evidence is overwhelming. The Lord lives. Praise Him.

True Peace Is Only In Christ

It is easy to recite a litany of the world's troubles. Jesus said that we would hear of wars and rumors of war, famines and earthquakes in various places. Besides these are the myriad of social ills, redefining marriage, killing our children, polluting our world, etc. We apply our technologies, our smart weapons, our years of learning, but the problems persist. We like to point to our progress, but we fight the same problems century after century, only with a modern veneer. The only progress possible is progress in the human heart, and only Jesus can bring that about. An article in a newsletter I receive monthly pointed out how we lift up democracy as the solution to the problems of nations around the world, but saying that democracy only works when it has a basis in the Christian Gospel. Human solution accomplish very little apart from the acknowledgment that Jesus is Lord over all. Until Christ returns the world will not be at peace. But until He returns we can have His peace as we allow Him to touch and change our hearts. The world's ills will remain with us, but be of good cheer, Jesus has overcome the world. ^(John 16:33) And that begins with the world in us.

Jesus, Contrary to the World

Jesus is disturbing! This began with the incarnation. God entered this world in the baby Jesus and Herod tried to kill Him. Jesus became the dividing line in all human history. Just as God confronted Adam and Even in the Garden they hid themselves from His presence, His holiness confronted their sin. Jesus changes things. He changes hearts, and we would rather be left alone. Jesus said of Himself that the world "hates Me because I testify of it, that its deeds are evil." (John 7:7) Whether it was in the Garden, or during Jesus ministry, or with any of those who have followed Him in the centuries since, where Jesus is presence there will be opposition. "Indeed, all who desire to live godly in Christ Jesus will be persecuted." (2 Timothy 2:12) That opposition tears crosses off of churches and destroys church buildings. Governments fear people reading the Bible because it is a book about Jesus. Yes, Jesus is disturbing because Jesus seeks to change human hearts and bring them into fellowship with Almighty God. Yet when we realize the joy, beauty, and peace He opens for us He truly is worth any cost that might come. He truly is the "pearl of great price".

Do We Have Idols?

There are numerous places in Scripture that speak against worshiping idols. Psalm 135 for example says, "The idols of the nations are but silver and gold, The work of man's hands. They have mouths, but they do not speak; They have eyes, but they do not see; They have ears, but they do not hear, Nor is there any breath at all in their mouths. Those who make them will be like them, Yes, everyone who trusts in them." [vss.15-18] This is speaking of actual statues that are worshiped, but there are numerous other things that can become idols. The question, as the psalmist states, is in what do we trust - our own strength, our mental ability, our wealth, our status? All of these can become idols. Scripture continually tells us to trust God and not be afraid. We do trust God, but somehow it is hard for us not to have a backup plan if God doesn't come through the way we want. Let's face it trusting God is hard. But where we have put at least some of our trust in our Lord we have seen Him work. We have seen things come together in our unplanned ways. We don't need idols. Our God is sufficient.

OUR FALLEN NATURE

How we are plagued by Romans chapter seven! This is the description of Paul's struggle with his own flesh, but it is applicable to us all. "For what I want to do I do not do, but what I hate I do."(Romans 7:15) When one desires to live in a way that pleases the Lord this is the struggle we face. It is proof of the sinful nature that resides within us. But the problem is still deeper. Paul says that he does what he does not want to do. In reality, that sinful nature really does want what we knows is wrong. This is the source of our battle with sin. "In my inner being I delight in God's law; but I see another law at work in the members of my body, waging war against the law of my mind"(Romans 7:22-23) Each of us must see this truth working in our own lives. We each know the sins we struggle with. We realize that we really do want that which we know is not pleasing to God. In this realization we cry out with St. Paul, "Who will rescue me from this body of death?"(Romans 7:24) It is when we are truly aware of this struggle that we can also shout, "Thanks be to God through Jesus Christ our Lord!" In Christ alone is our hope. His work on the cross has taken our punishment, granting us forgiveness and new life in turning to Him.

GREAT TRUTH IN SIMPLE EXPRESSIONS

We teach children the simple table grace, "God is great, God is good, and we thank Him for our food." Simple, maybe even a bit simplistic for adults, but it is also profound. God is great! There is none greater, omnipotent, omniscient, and omnipresent. He is creator of all things. He made us and all that is. He gives us every breath that we take. If He made us He also has shown us the best way in which we can live. God is good! He is a Father, our Father, who always seeks the best for us, and uses all things for our good. He is not just The Force out there somewhere. He knows and cares about each one of us personally. We could go on for many lines about His greatness and goodness, and we should in our own times of prayer and meditation. Because of all of this, He is due our overwhelming thanks. Not just for food, but for everything that comes to us. Maybe we need to remind ourselves again about the simple things we teach our children. They really are true.

Our Attitude Of Humble Service

I've said that there are lessons to be learned about our Lord from everything that is around us. From the small creatures God has created to the encounters we have with people each day. From my personal need or visiting patients as a pastor I've seen much of the work of those in our local hospital. They offer a few more lessons, and not just on health issues. The staff is great. The nurses are committed, and very capable, but the ones that impress me are the nursing assistants, down to the housekeeping lady that does the floors. They are the ones that get the nastiness jobs, from taking out the trash to cleaning up people's messes. I'm sure they don't always like each task, but they do it with a smile and a wonderful attitude of service. They carry an attitude of humility and a desire to serve. I am reminded of Jesus words that He, the author of all life, God Himself, "came not to be served but to serve and give His life as a ransom for many." It is beautiful when we see it in others, and it points us to The One who is the example of humble, self-giving service.

LOOKING INSIDE

Medical people have many means of looking inside us. There are CT scans, MRIs, X-rays and numerous kind of probes with camera and lights. There are also the blood and other tests that tell what is happening inside. Doctors need to see inside as best they can in order to treat us effectively. But then what does God look at? He searches our hearts and our minds. He sees us to the depth our being. (I Chronicles 28:8) He is called the "master builder" or in this case the Master Doctor. He says, "I know the plans I have for you..." (Jeremiah 29:11) Our doctors seek, to heal us so that we have a good quality of life, and are able to pursue those good tasks in life. Our God sees us far more deeply, working to fulfill His eternal plan and our place in His Kingdom. He works in us for a good life of service now, and for eternity. See. You can learn lessons from our Lord wherever He places you. Let's just be open and listen.

Do We Believe God?

Do we believe God? Notice I didn't ask if we believe IN God. The majority of people in this country say they do - in whatever form they conceive of Him. But I'm asking do we believe God? Do we believe what God tells us? We have the recorded revelation of His words in the Bible. One of the amazing things about His Scripture is that He shows the bad with the good. He doesn't sugarcoat the mess people get themselves into when they ignore His good will for their lives. We are to learn from their failures as well as His direct teachings for our good. But do we believe God? In too many instances the answer is No. We either have no knowledge of what is in between the Bible's covers, or pick and choose what we like and don't like, or rationalize them away by saying we have gained so much more knowledge today than they had. There are all kinds of ways we choose to ignore God's clear Word. The bottom like is that in many ways we simply do not believe God, and it is to our own detriment.

A Successful Life

When we are planning a road trip. We get out the map, looked at Google maps on line, and call a friend to ask their advice. We want to avoid heavy traffic, delays around major cities, etc. The trip will take a number of hours, and we would like it to be as pleasant as possible. Nothing new here. We all do the same. But what about the journey through life. We would like that to be as pleasant as possible also, but that takes even more planning. It is not a matter of just having enough income to be reasonably secure and comfortable. A truly successful journey through life doesn't depend upon wealth, but upon walking along with the One who designed our life, and holds it in His hands. The Prophet Micah said, "He has told you, O man, what is good; And what does the LORD require of you but to do justice, to love kindness, and to walk humbly with your God?" (Micah 6:8) Justice, kindness, and humility - a real road for a successful journey through life.

Finding God's Blessings

I try to read a portion of the New Testament and the Old Testament each morning. This morning's readings both spoke of the opposition to God's Word and will. The first was Paul on trial for preaching Jesus and the resurrection. The second was opposition against the Jews rebuilding the Temple in Jerusalem after the exile. I've been writing this week about God's will for us expressed in Holy Scripture. This also raises opposition. Our sinful nature hates to be told that we are wrong, that we are going in a wrong direction, that God, in fact, really does know better then we do how we should live. As I said on Monday we don't believe God. But whenever we are willing to accept any of the truth God has given we find that there is a blessing in doing so. God is a gracious and forgiving Lord. That was the work of our Lord Jesus on Calvary. He is willing to restore all who turn to Him, but we must turn to Him, and not just expect Him to bless whatever we think is right.

Blessings Within God's Will For Our Life

When Jesus hung on the cross He prayed for the very ones who were crucifying Him. "Father, forgive them for they know not what they are doing." They were ignorant of God's good purpose for their lives, and what He was doing for them in this sacrifice of His only begotten Son. In ignorance they were harming the very thing that was intended to give them life. This is Pride Month in our local community. Last weekend there was a great celebration of inclusiveness praising all those lifestyles that God has declared as wrong and destructive of the good He has established for our lives. God is merciful. He is always ready to forgive those who turn to Him. Jesus even prayed for those acting in ignorance, but that doesn't make it right. People are destroying so much of the good God wants for their lives. Throughout Scripture we see the truth that God's blessing comes with obedience, but also that His judgment comes with disobedience. Jesus' death and resurrection made it possible for all people to come and find true life in Him. And He has given us His Holy Word to be our guide. We would do well to take it seriously.

Our Refuge, Our Hope

Many passages in Scripture have been set to music. The whole book of Psalms is a hymnal. Many of our hymns are inspired by Bible passages. A number of Scripture choruses are used in contemporary worship services. There are many taken directly from the King James version. One that I particularly like is from Isaiah 61:3. He gave "them beauty for ashes, the oil of joy for mourning, the garment of praise for the spirit of heaviness; that they might be called trees of righteousness, the planting of the LORD, that he might be glorified." I'd like to sing it for you, but that probably wouldn't be a good idea. The Isaiah passage begins with the words, "To appoint unto them that mourn in Zion, to give unto them beauty..." We talk so much about the problems in our society as I did yesterday. We mourn over the loss of Godly values and the pain it has caused our world. But as this verse say our refuge, our hope is in the Lord who promises to changes ashes into beauty, and ultimately all to His glory. This is a song worth singing.

Our Weakness

As I get older I realize the things I can no longer do and where I am very much dependent upon others. In the physical realm that is a hard lesson learn. But it is a good lesson regardless of our age. Think about what Paul said in II Corinthians 12:10. "For when I am weak, then I am strong." Paul had been persecuted, mocked, beaten, jailed. Much of his freedom denied him. This made him look beyond himself for a strength he didn't have. His eyes had to turn to the Lord Christ who alone could support him, guide him, and give him the strength he needed for the situations he faced. No one likes to be weak, and we are supposed to use all of the physical strength and ability our Lord gave us. We use it in service to His glory. But at the same time we accept our need for support, wisdom, and guidance from One beyond ourselves. We, in fact, rejoice in our weakness because that maintains our bond to the true source of our life and strength. When we realize that we are weak in ourselves then we can become strong in Jesus.

HAPPINESS AND FEELING GOOD ISN'T EVERYTHING

Are you happy today? Tha's really a poor question to ask. It is completely subjective, and dependent upon the circumstances of any given time. A better question is, Are you content? When understood from the point of view of our faith in Jesus Christ we can say yes I'm content. With the Apostle Paul we can say, "I have learned to be content in whatever circumstances I am. ... in any and every circumstance I have learned the secret of being filled and going hungry, both of having abundance and suffering need. ... I can do all things through Him who strengthens me." (Philippians 4:11-13) It is nice to be happy, and by God's abundant grace we have many happy times in life. But we also know that trials and stresses come. We face some difficult even tragic circumstances. Yet we are never left alone by God. It is He who strengthens us. This is not ignoring the present circumstance, but drawing on Christ's guidance and strength to move forward. We also know that in Jesus Christ this circumstance is not the final word. In Him there is more and it is good.

God At The Center

I am recently retired and have a little more free time. What do I do with it? What is God's will for me in this time of life? These are valid questions that I'm sure the Good Lord will answer as the days go on. But there is an important answer for all of us to the question "what is God will for me?" Paul writing to the Thessalonian Church said, "Rejoice always; pray without ceasing; in everything give thanks; for this is God's will for you in Christ Jesus."(I Thess. 5:16-18) Rejoice, pray, give thanks - that is to be the content of our lives. It is from this that all else will flow. God will reveal any specific direction He desires, but this is where we begin. We rejoice because the Lord has redeemed us. No circumstances of life will change that. We come to Him many time a day in prayer. In fact, our life is lived in a continual relationship of conversation with Him. We give thanks in everything because God works in everything for our good, even when it doesn't look very good. We really don't need to fret about knowing God's will. This is a life that witnesses to the abundance of His grace.

And For Our People

We know what it means to repent for our sins, but how about repenting for the sins of all people? Really? Many would say that doesn't make sense. We don't have control over anyone but ourselves and our own actions. Yet many of the great prayers in the Bible made this type of confession. In the small Old Testament book of Nehemiah we hear him pray, "let Your ear now be attentive and Your eyes open to hear the prayer of Your servant which I am praying before You now, day and night, on behalf of the sons of Israel Your servants, confessing the sins of the sons of Israel which we have sinned against You; I and my father's house have sinned."(Nehemiah 1:6) In this prayer there is a refusal to separate one's self from the rest of the community. It is so easy to point fingers at those sinners over there. We are not as bad as they are, but sin is sin. My "small" sin separates me from God just as much as their "big" sins. I've written in the past about my opposition to certain accepted practices in today's society. But I also realize that I'm as guilty before God as anyone else. A prayer of repentance for all doesn't accept evil as normal and good, but it implores God to open all of our hearts to receive the love He freely gives and to change us all more into His image.

The Place Where We Belong

When one is away from home on vacation or for whatever reason there is always a sense of it being temporary, along with a longing to be home. It really doesn't matter how necessary the away stay is or how good a time one is having, it is still not home. There is a longing for the settled, the familiar, the perminent. The place where one belongs. We are told that when Abraham was called to leave the place where he was living to go toward the Promised Land that he understood he was ultimately "looking forward to the city with foundations, whose architect and builder is God."(Hebrews 11:9) Nothing in this life is permanent. Nothing here is exactly as we would like it to be regardless of how many resources we have to try to make it that way. There is a longing for the permanent home, the place where we really belong in perfect fellowship with our Lord, "longing for a better country—a heavenly one."(vs.16) We have a very real task to do while we are here summed up in the second great commandment, to love our neighbor as ourselves. But our ultimate longing is for the place where we truly belong, our home in perfect harmony with our Lord. All other longings are just pointing forward to that.

OUR LIFE - AN ADVERTISEMENT

Publicity is a major industry today. Every organization of any size depends upon it to spread the word about whatever it is they do. Products must be publicized to be sold. A few years ago a 30 second TV ads during the Super Bowl this year cost eight million dollars. I have no idea what it is today. Political candidates spend millions of dollars to publicize their agenda in order to get elected. Churches publicize their programs to get people to come. There is a hymn we sing that proclaims, "I love to tell the story of Jesus and His love." You and I have been given the greatest message in the world, greater than any product, candidate, or program. It's cost was far greater then any Super Bowl ad, but not in dollars. We have the Good News of eternal salvation in Jesus Christ. This is a message that every human being needs to hear. We can't reach every human being, but we can reach those that we meet each day. By our life, and our words, we can publicize this Good News. So, whether you knew it or not, you really are in the publicity business, too.

Jesus' Challenge

People go to all kinds of lengths for excitement and challenges. I understand that a record has been set for the most bungy jumps in a short period of time, and another for the number of back flips across a football field. Certainly not something I ever would have considered trying. Even so it highlight something in our nature that craves a challenge, that thrives on excitement, and that desires to be singled out for a good accomplishment. Being a part of the nature God created, these desires are not wrong. The problem with so much of mankind is that we seek fulfillment in the wrong places. The Lord offers us all of these in His service. If you read the Gospels, the life Jesus is offering His followers is a constant challenge. A life of faith comes with no guarantees for an easy time, and without any knowledge of what is ahead. We enter a walk with the Lord where His central instruction simply says "follow Me and trust Me". From here He takes us in directions we never dreamed, but if we are willing to follow His path we will hear the only commendation that really matters, "Well done good and faithful servant.".

LEAVE VENGEANCE TO THE LORD

Probably the hardest instruction Jesus ever gave His followers was to "love your enemies, do good to those who hate you".^(Luke 6:27) Paul repeats this same instruction in writing to the Roman church "never pay back evil for evil to anyone...never take your own revenge, beloved, but leave room for the wrath God, for it is written 'vengeance is mine, I will repay, says the Lord'...do not be overcome by evil but overcome evil with good."^(Luke12:17-21) Forgiving someone who has hurt us is so hard. It strikes us as unfair. We hurt and they get off easy. But the issue before God is not so much what the other person did. He will deal with that in His own way. The issue is what unforgiveness, anger, and bitterness does in our own hearts. It festers and puts a block between ourselves and our Lord. To forgive someone who has hurt us doesn't say that what they did was right. It simply gives up the power to judge, and puts it in God's hands. Even without the other person asking our forgiveness we refuse to let anything take root in our hearts that separates us from our Lord. Hard, yes, but the right thing to do, and the way to our own peace with God.

Memorial Day

We set aside a Memorial Day each year to honor the men and women who serve and have served in our military. Last evening we watched the Memorial Day program from our national capital. It was a moving presentation with numerous stories of sacrifice and selfless service in the cause of freedom. It is right to honor such service. Yet, at the same time it should cause us to long and pray for the time when such service is no longer needed. The Prophet Isaiah wrote, "In the last days the mountain of the LORD's temple will be established as the highest of the mountains; it will be exalted above the hills, and all nations will stream to it. Many peoples will come and say, 'Come, let us go up to the mountain of the LORD, to the temple of the God of Jacob. He will teach us his ways, so that we may walk in his paths.' The law will go out from Zion, the word of the LORD from Jerusalem. He will judge between the nations and will settle disputes for many peoples. They will beat their swords into plowshares and their spears into pruning hooks. Nation will not take up sword against nation, nor will they train for war anymore."(Isaiah 2:2-4) National leaders have many times quoted these last two sentences in their speeches. Their efforts alone will not bring it about. Only our Lord Jesus will be able to fulfill this promise. Let us pray that He come quickly.

Enfolded In Beauty

When a person sees a beautiful sight we sometimes hear the expression "it is breathtaking". There is a sense of awe and wonder concerning the experience. I have a CD recording of Mozart's Ave Verum that I will sometimes play through my computer while I'm working. I don't understand the words of the composition but the music and vocals are wonderful. I've been in groups of Christians singing a majestic hymn of our faith. At times its beauty has been so great I've had to stop singing and let the sound surround me with its wonder. I hope you can identify with this in one form or another. It is more than an emotional experience. It is being enveloped in a beauty beyond words. We can't live in those experiences continually while on earth, but I think they are windows that God gives us for a brief look into the Glory of His kingdom. This is a small glimpse into the glory that awaits all who are in Christ Jesus.

Transformed By Glory

The Apostle Paul wrote about the abundance of visions and revelations he had received from the Lord. Yesterday I wrote about the glimpses of God's glory we sometimes receive through music. Paul wrote to the Roman church that what can be known of God is clearly seen in the things He has made. (Romans 1:19-20) Maybe it is though the marvel of the cosmos, or the astounding complexity of the human body, or the wonder of why God created mankind, we are allowed these small windows into the very Kingdom of God. They are marvelous experience, but as I said yesterday we can't live there all the time. We have our daily tasks and challenges in this fallen world. But those glimpses, those windows, do affect all that we do now. By having even a small look into God's Kingdom it deepens our love for God and our love for our neighbor. These are the two great commandments. Writing to the Corinthians Paul said that we "beholding as in a mirror the glory of the Lord, are being transformed into the same image from glory to glory..."(2Corinthians 3:18) This is not a point for our own pride, but a deepened desire to draw all others into that same glory.

There Is No Comparison

One more thought about the glimpses or windows into God's Kingdom that I mentioned the last two days. It is important to see the awesome wonder, majesty, and glory of God whether through the Scriptures or the things of life. When we compare the things we treasure now, and especially the things that satisfy our fleshly desire, the things of this life look very pale and secondary. It is not that earthly things are unimportant, but in light of the glory of our God to which we are called, they are seen in a completely different way. This is especially true of the temptations to sin that touch us all. Seeing the riches of God's glory we are strengthened to resist those temptations. We will never be completely free of earthly desires, and that is not bad. It is here that we live, work, and serve. But we live in the light of God's glory now and always.

LIFE IS A BUMPY RIDE

In John 16:33 Jesus said "In this world you will have trouble." We really don't like that, but it is a fact of life in our fallen world. We are subject to the trials and ills that sin has wrought. Sometimes things are of our own doing, but often from events beyond our control. It is not God's punishment, but he has allowed it along with the promise that He is in the midst of it with us. When Moses was recounting the history of Israel in the 40 years of wandering before they entered the Promised Land, he said to them, "Remember how the LORD your God led you all the way in the desert these forty years, to humble you and to test you in order to know what was in your heart..." (Deuteronomy 8:2) The mystery of why evil is allowed will be with us until we are fully in God presence in the Kingdom. We can't say that every trial is punishment, or even for our need to be humbled. What every time of trial does, however, is present us with the choice of giving in to self-pity and despair, or clinging to God in trust. Life will never go along as smooth and trouble free as we would like, but we do put our trust in our Lord who walks every path with us. And there are many lessons to be learned along the way.

KEEP THE GOAL IN SIGHT

I've always enjoyed exploring the rivers off of Maryland's Chesapeake Bay. When going out of Sandy Point on the western side, the Bay is about four miles wide. On a clear day you can see across the Bay to the mouth of the Chester River a bit to the north. We would pick a spot on the far shore and head toward it. Sometimes the water was a bit choppy, there were always crab trap lines to watch out for, and one time we ran into a sudden downpour. But as long as we kept that spot on the far shore in view we would get to where we wanted to be. The image has an obvious analogy for life. We are traveling a distance measured in years. The path has its share of choppy water and obstacles. We have learned that our hope is in the Lord, and His truth is the way to life. Sometimes the way seems very clouded, we don't feel that the Lord is near, and conditions of life don't make sense. It is just at such times that we keep our eyes fixed on that which we know to be true. We keep our hope set on Jesus. We will reach the far shore.

THE NARROW DOOR

"Make every effort", Jesus tells his listeners, "to enter through the narrow door". (Luke 23:24) Our God is a God of great love and extreme mercy. His grace extends to all mankind. But we must never be causal about, or presume upon, that mercy. How often have we heard, "Oh a loving God would never..." I believe God's mercy is very wide, and there will be many in heaven that we do not expect, but we who have been given the truth of God's love in Jesus Christ are called to live in that truth each day. This is not living by some set of rules, but by never wanting to compromise, deny, or make light of the relationship we have with the Lord. Just as our earthly relationships are important, we want to do nothing to harm them. It is even more so with our Lord. Jesus is the source of our life. He is the narrow door, and through Him we have the greatest life possible.

A Reflected Light

There has been a focus on the moon in these last few weeks since this is the 50th anniversary month of the first astronauts walking on the surface of the moon. It was striking to me last evening that there was a bright full moon illuminating the sky. The thought was also raised about the moon in our men's Bible study last evening. How are we like the moon? Think about it. As bright as the moon was last night we realize that it has no natural light of its own. It only reflects the light it receives from the sun. OK, now how are we like the moon? We have no natural light of our own - we really don't. All that is good is only a reflection of the Son. By the grace of God the life of Christ works in us by the presence of His Spirit. His nature of love, joy, peace, patience, kindness, meekness, gentleness, faith, and self-control, the fruit of God's Spirit ^(Galatians 5:22-23), grows in our lives as we seek to be a part of Him. It is that we are reflecting to others when any good comes forth from us. So with all the moon talk this month keep in mind that you and I are called to be like the moon illuminating our world with what we receive from our Lord Jesus.

Our Heritage

We get tongue tied trying to pronounce some of the biblical names, especially in the Old Testament. The Bible spends quite a number of pages on listing genealogies. It was quite important to the Jews. This has been a fascinating subject for many today, as well. Some people take great pride in the fact that they descended from some famous person. The Pharisees of Jesus day were very proud that they were descendants of Abraham, but Jesus topped them all. He said, "before Abraham was born, I AM." [John 8:58] He existed before all mankind. He is God. Our own lineage can be interesting. But when we are born of water and the Spirit in baptism [see John 3:5] our lineage is immediately traced to Jesus. Not only is He our direct ancestor, He is our living Brother today. No one can be in a better family than that.

REMOVE THE MIXTURE

There was a body of Christian believers in the city of Corinth. Now Corinth was a cosmopolitan city and an important trading center in the Roman world. It was known throughout the empire as an immoral city. The new Christians had a difficult time giving up some of their old habits and practices. At the end of chapter four of Paul's first letter to these believers he had to ask, "What do you desire? Shall I come to you with a rod, or with love and a spirit of gentleness?"[(I Cor.4:21)] Obviously they wanted the love and gentleness, but for some they also wanted to continue their old practices as well. Sound very contemporary to me. However, Paul went on to say that they couldn't have it both ways. He had to rebuke them harshly for a number of their practices. There is a verse repeated twice in the book of Proverbs that tells us "There is a way which seems right to a man, But its end is the way of death." God came to give us life, but as Paul was trying to show the Corinthians, that life is found in a way that brings honor to our God. God has given us forgiveness and new life in Jesus Christ. This is a grace gift beyond measure. Paul calls us to rejoice in the new that has been so graciously given.

Our God Be Praised

The shortest psalm among all of the 150 in the Book of Psalms is number 117. "Praise the LORD, all you nations; extol him, all you peoples. For great is his love toward us, and the faithfulness of the LORD endures forever. Praise the LORD." Only two verses but the greatest of expressions that if truly followed by all nations would reveal the greatest measure of God's grace upon all peoples. The word LORD when printed in capitals is the word Yah in Hebrew, the one true God, the creator of the heavens and the earth. It is before Him that we are all called to humbly bow. It is this God who loves us, and has shown His faithfulness throughout our lives. It is this God who has worked through all the centuries since creation to form a people for a living and eternal relationship with Himself. It is this God, our God, who has shown Himself faithful even in the midst of our unfaithfulness. It is this God who is the Creator, Redeemer, and Sanctifier of all mankind. Our God is worthy of all praise. Praise the Lord.

WE ARE NOT POST MODERNISTS

We are told that we live in a "post modern" age. I always thought that was a curious term. It seems like an oxymoron to me. But what is more important is the definition placed on postmodernism which does define our age. "At its heart, postmodernism posits that neither revelation nor reason can give us the story of reality. In fact, according to postmodernism, there is no universal, discernible story of reality. Truth is a social construct for the postmodernist, even observable truths like male and female." This age says that there is no absolute truth and "neither revelation or reason" can provide us with a solid foundation for life. As biblically centered Christians we find ourselves completely at odds with such an understanding of life. The postmodern understanding essentially puts any acknowledgment of God as our creator, and the One who established the way of life for His creation, completely out of the picture. Thus we find ourselves at odds with the postmodern view of life. We are called to live our lives by the absolute truth in which we believe. This has led to strong opposition in various areas of life, but then it always has. Even so, that is our calling, and on God's revelation we must stand.

Rejection Without Knowledge[1]

Yesterday I wrote about our post modern culture, its rejection of all absolutes, and our need to stand firm on the witness of Holy Scripture. The Europeans are ahead of us in this rejection, but not by much. In a publication from the C.S.Lewis Institute I read the following. "Increasingly, Europeans are devoted to a different religion - a militant form of secularism that sees the Christian history as a time of darkness and oppression - a time to be not just forgotten, but intentionally abandoned. Yet how many of those who desecrate churches and vandalize religious monuments even know what it is they're attacking? How much could those who dumped rainbow paint on the Reformers in Geneva tell us about them, other than they were Christians...or men?" This is increasingly the nature of our post-modern, post-christian world while we seek to hold on to truths revealed more than 3000 years ago. At times it seems a futile struggle, but God gave us a promise. "My word which goes forth from My mouth; It will not return to Me empty, Without accomplishing what I desire, And without succeeding in the matter for which I sent it." And if one is willing to look, there are evidences of that accomplishment in numerous places on the earth. We are encouraged. God will accomplish His purpose for creation in spite of all opposition.

What Is Real Power?

We are impressed with powerful things - a great earth mover, 400 horsepower under the hood, a football team's front four, military might, and so on. Our young grandson loves to pretend he is one of the current superhero characters. We certainly believe that our God is all powerful. He can do anything He chooses, any time He chooses. But He always has a habit of turning our concepts of reality up side down. We think in terms of force and might. God doesn't. The greatest power of God is displayed in His love, and in forgiveness, His care for all people. He has shown it to us by the bloody body of His Son hanging on a cross. Self giving love and forgiveness have the power to change hearts, heal long festering wounds, and mend relationships. People need to see that kind of power displayed in the Church. Love and forgiveness can change us and those around us for all eternity. No earthly power can do that.

God, Our Creator, Our Redeemer, Our Sanctifier

I have written often about God as the author and source of life, and His breathing life into us. When I do, it often brings up the debate about creation vs. evolution. I'm not all that concerned about there being billions of years of the cosmos' existence. I don't know what happened to this 8000 mile diameter ball of rock we live on before God said, "let there be light" bringing order out of chaos. What I do express as an essential truth of our faith is that we did not come from some lower form of life, and that, at some point in time past, we were created by God, complete and without sin. And further, it was from this sinless initial state, that we later rebelled from the will of our God, becoming estranged from Him ever since. If it were not true that we began in a sinless relationship with our Creator, and later broke that relationship by our rebellion, there would be no need for a Redeemer, and the whole of Scripture becomes reduced to ancient history topped off with a few moral lessons. This, tragically, is the way many treat God's Word today. The message we declare in Jesus Christ is that, apart from Him, we are eternally separated from our Creator. By His gracious sacrificial act, we have been redeemed and restored to our Lord. Understanding this helps us make sense of today's life, and gives us a sense of direction and a reason for hope.

Our Great Hope

There is a song sung by one of the prominent men's Gospel quartets that talks about the conditions of our times. The chorus ends with the line, "but I've read the back of the book and we win". We don't need a singing group to tell us about our times. The news glares at us from every newspaper and broadcast. We live in the midst of it. Yesterday I wrote about the work of our God in the creation and redemption of mankind. That is the work of our gracious Father God to bring people - you and me - to a place of peace and harmony with Himself. He has worked for us over centuries of time. He has promised never to leave or forsake us, and to complete the good purpose He has for our lives. In the difficulties of our days and the tragedies we hear about daily, yet there is hope. We are strengthened to continue day by day with our eyes fixed on the promise of our Lord, and the evidence we have seen in our Redeemer. We have the greatest reason for hope.

Are You Satisfied?

The opening line of Psalm 108 says, "My heart is satisfied, O God." I think that's a wonderful expression. There are many things we would like to see happen in life. There are many things we plan and strive for. Motivational experts tell us it is necessary to set goals in life. All of that is fine, but above it all, our ultimate satisfaction is in our God. If nothing else ever comes to fruition, we can still be satisfied that our God has called us to be in fellowship with Himself. The priests of ancient Israel were not given an inheritance of land with the rest of the Israelites. God said to them, "I am your portion and your inheritance."(Numbers18:20) God knows we need the basic things of life, and He provides them. It is fine to work toward the things we desire. But our God is our portion in this life, and in Him we can be satisfied.

FATHERS ARE IMPORTANT

They say, "like father, like son". I can remember when I was a kid, I wanted to be where my dad was and doing what he was doing. If he was out in the yard, that's where I wanted to be. I learned how to splice an electrical wire from him, and to change a wall outlet. We did a number of basic carpentry things together. Dad took the family to church each week, and led the music in the Sunday School room. What was important to my father was important to me. What he didn't particularly care about, sports in particular, neither did I. Like father, like son. All of this is to emphasize the importance of the leadership role a father plays in the life of his children, both sons and daughters. It is the only place they really learn what a man is supposed to be. Above all, a father is to be a man of faith leading his family into the only lasting values that truly matter. All of the fun times will one day be only memories. All of the financial security is a passing and shallow comfort. What last is that which gives them hope and security in Jesus. That is the lasting legacy fathers have to give.

Humility

Humility is usually not a highly valued human characteristic. We look more to strength and good self esteem. People often see humility as weakness, and we certainly don't want that. The very nature of our political and corporate system requires self promotion. To get ahead we must show that we are better than others. The Apostle Paul, however, writes just the opposite. "Do nothing out of selfish ambition or vain conceit, but in humility consider others better than yourselves." (Philippians 2:3) This, he says, is the very nature of Jesus that we are to emulate. This is not weakness. We are to use our talents and abilities to the fullest. It is possible to accomplish many good things, but do them with no real thought about ourselves, but to the glory of God and for the good of others. Whether an artist or a bricked layer, an accountant or stock clerk, we work with thanksgiving to the fullest of our God-given ability, and give Him glory for it all. According to Jesus, it is when we are willing to live in humility before God that He exalts us. As we humble ourselves in service to others, we have God's esteem, and that is far better than self-esteem.

Careful But Not Fearful

We hear so much these days about gun violence. 30+ people killed in random shootings just a couple of weeks ago. There are renewed calls for gun control. These tragedies have been in places of employment, in shopping malls, and even in churches. They are horrible, and leave many individual devastations in their wake. One article pointed out, however, that statistically each of us has a very low probability of being involved in such an incident. I'm not sure how comforting that is, but the article did say that we can't live our lives in fear. We have responsibilities, and normal patterns of life with work, shopping, entertainment, and so forth. We can't and shouldn't curtail these activities out of fear. Above all we believe in our God who is a part of us at all times, our God who cares about every soul of the victims and even of the shooters. He has allowed sinful mankind to make choices, and at times those choices are used in very wrong ways. Yet He is not absent. He is present to calm our fears, to comfort the bereaved, and He alone is the One with power to touch hearts and overcome hate. Some aspects of gun control are important, but our main concern, and the focus of our prayers, is for God to change sinful hearts, including our own. And above all that He would shorten the days until Christ's return. (Mark 13:20) He alone will bring the peace we all want.

Symbols of Holiness

Last evening I was reading in the Old Testament book of Leviticus. Yes, that's the book most people avoid with its tedious recording of all the Jewish laws. And I admit it can be tedious reading. Even further we know that in Christ we are freed from the strict adherence to the Jewish legal system. Nonetheless the book is instructive. In the 8th chapter we read of Moses consecrating the priests for their service in the Tabernacle. The text speaks of each of the holy garments the priest wore, the white robe, the sacred breastpiece with the sacred stones called Urim and Thummim, the turban, and the anointing oil poured on their heads. So what has all this to do with us? It speaks to the sacredness of the office of priest or pastor. This is a holy calling to serve God's people. There is a sacred consecration in Christ. Oh, we don't follow all the Mosaic rituals, but that doesn't change the sacredness of the task God has given our spiritual leaders. But even further, Scripture tells us that we all have a priestly calling through faith in the Lord Jesus Christ. Whether tradesman, or office worker, retired or homebound, we all have been given the same consecration through our baptism into Christ. We are all called to minister God's grace in the place of our calling. We probably won't have sacred oil poured on our heads, but the holiness of the Levitical calling is still upon us. We serve in the joy of our Lord.

THE RITUALS TEACH IMPORTANT LESSONS

Yesterday I used the theme in one chapter of the book of Leviticus. This book, even though it is rather tedious to read through, is part of the Lord's Word, and He gave it for the good of His people. It is certainly true that we are not bound by the law. Jesus fulfilled the law perfectly. However, as with many things in the Old Testament, they point forward as types of things that were fulfilled for us in the salvation work of Jesus Christ. The many blood sacrifices, for example, point to the necessity of our Lord's blood shed in atonement for our sins. The people were instructed to bring an unblemished clean animal as an offering to the Lord. Unblemished as in the perfect sinless life of Jesus. Many verses deal with the proper way to present offerings. The root of the Hebrew word for offering means "to draw near". It is what God desires in all of His instructions, that we draw near to Him, and has shown us the way. No, Leviticus is not a "fun" book to read, but there is much in it showing how our Lord continually reaches out in grace to draw people to Himself.

THE ROCK

I am a creature of habit. I do things at a certain time. I put things is certain places. A crooked picture on the wall bothers me. Obviously I like order, certainty, things that can be counted on. But we live in a disordered, and uncertain world. The Psalmist faced this disorder over and over. They often cried out for help in the midst of things that were going awry. But they came back time and again to what they knew was solid. "I trust in your unfailing love; my heart rejoices in your salvation." [Psalm13:5] We try as best we can to make our solid places and safe havens in our world, but there is truly only one place, one person that is solid and unchanging. "In you, LORD, I have taken refuge; let me never be put to shame. In your righteousness, rescue me and deliver me; turn your ear to me and save me. Be my rock of refuge, to which I can always go;..." [Psalm71:1-3] Our ultimate hope is in God alone. He will not fail us.

Unseen Care

We have a plant in our living room that I was given when I had my stay in the hospital a while back. I've enjoyed watching it go through various cycles of its growth. It came with one bloom which lasted for a while before dying off. That was followed by seven lovely blooms. They now are dying, and at present there don't seem to any new ones following, just large green leaves. It strikes me that its cycles are not unlike those of human life itself, and I'm thinking about my life in particular. There, too, are various cycles. Some more beautiful than others. Some flowering, others pretty ordinary, or even at times painful. But there is one thing consistent with the plant. In whatever part of its cycle, I have to take care of it. It needs regular watering, and occasionally having the dead leaves removed. In our lives we are subject to our gracious Lord who is present through all of our cycles of life, and works for us in each time. The plant has no concept of what I'm doing to improve its life, and often we can't see the work of our Lord. Yet it continues nonetheless. The purpose of the plant is to bring beauty and joy to our home. That is no less the purpose we have in the world we occupy.

USING GOD-GIVEN GIFTS

We admire men and women who have made it to the top of their profession, especially if they came from a poor background and worked their way up. They are sometimes referred to as self-made individuals, but there really is no such thing. Yes, they had to put forth great effort, endure hardship, and have patience as they moved forward, but where did all that come from? It is God who has made us, and we are His. He has given us personality traits, A, B, C types, or whatever. It is He who has given us gifts and abilities in certain areas. It is He who has open or closed doors of opportunity. Self-made? Not a chance. And this is true for each of us. God has given you gifts just as He has with corporate climbers. Your gifts are no less important. Your accomplishments don't need to be compared to anyone. We are responsible before God to recognize the gifts God has given, and use them to the fullest to His glory. Whether one is the best industry CEO, able to preach a great sermon, or skilled in making a solid brick wall, it is our gift from God and used to bring Him honor. (Mark12:41-44)

LIVING BY THE RIGHT STANDARD

What is the standard by which we guide our lives? This question is both personal and extends into the larger sphere of governments and nations. While many of the Founding Fathers of our country were not Christian in the strictest sense, they did acknowledge a natural law established by God, and they knew and revered the Bible. That became the standard by which they chose to establish a government. Unfortunately, that standard is no longer recognized. Today we find ourselves in the place of ancient Israel when they did not acknowledge the sovereignty of God over their whole people. Twelve time in one context or another the statement is repeated, "In those days there was no king in Israel; every man did what was right in his own eyes." (Judges 17:6) The writer of Proverbs follows this with an important comment. "The way of a fool is right in his own eyes, But a wise man is he who listens to counsel." (Proverbs 12:15) The only true and sure counsel is the revealed Word of God which, until recent centuries, had been the acknowledged standard for life. What we see today are people and nations living as fools by doing only what is right in their own eyes. I don't believe this is going to change until our Lord returns, but can only say, as individual believers in the Lord Jesus Christ, it must not be so for us.

OUR TRIALS DO NOT STOP GOD'S WORK

When one begins a project, whether it is a large building in the heart of a city, or a wood working project in a small shop, there are always a few unforeseen difficulties that crop up. The worker or workers must consider other ways to solve the difficulty and complete the project. Such has been the case of God completing the purpose for which He created mankind. God had an intimate relationship with man and woman in the Garden, but their rebellion separated them and caused God to begin His costly plan of redemption. At the Exodus God brought the people out of Egypt and could have led them to the Promised Land within six months, but they rebelled and God had to lead them through forty years in the wilderness. The Prophet Isaiah wrote, "Behold, the LORD'S hand is not so short that it cannot save; Nor is His ear so dull that it cannot hear. But your iniquities have made a separation between you and your God..." (Isaiah 59:1-2) We can and do delay God's good purpose for us by our sins, but the marvelous truth of God's grace is that He will not let us go. His forgiveness and cleansing are always available. Paul wrote to the Philippines, "He who began a good work in you will carry it on to completion until the day of Christ Jesus." (Philippiens1:6) Like any good builder, God will not stop work until His project is completed to perfection.

History Is Important

I have been working on our church records of pastoral acts (weddings, funerals, etc.) that go back over forty years. I want to get them in better and more concise form. Its been an interesting project bringing back many memories of past action in our ministry. There were many learning experiences along the way. We really are a product of our past, and hopefully that has brought some maturity and wisdom into the present. This project has required that I take a look into my past. This is all personal history for me, but it does point to the importance of not forgetting what has gone on before. History is important. Now, having said all that, it brings us back to Scripture. The Bible is really a record of our history. It is not a bunch of old unrelated stories, but one record from Genesis through Revelation of God brining us into being and continually working through many years to bring us into a full relationship with Himself. That is why it is important to understand the whole story of the Bible. It is our story just as my forty years of church records are my smaller part of the story. Don't neglect the Scripture. It offers you wisdom, maturity, and new life in the present.

A REAL LIVING PERSON

Who is this God we believe in? What is He like? God is not just out there somewhere, a power we call on occasionally when we are in need. He is not just the Force, as in Star Wars. God is a rational person who desires that we learn to know Him. When Paul was speaking to the philosophers in Athens, he said that God created mankind "so that they would seek him and perhaps reach out for him and find him, though he is not far from any one of us."(Acts 17:27) This is an amazing truth that is stated throughout our Scriptures. Our sins have made a separation between us, but that has not changed God's desire for us to know and draw near to Him. He has perfectly revealed Himself to us in Jesus Christ. He once said to Philip, "anyone who has seen me has seen the Father."(John 14:9) God has come to us in Jesus. He has done everything necessary for us to know and have a relationship with Him, but He will not force Himself on us. He invites us to come, to read His Word, to become quiet before Him, to think, and to pray. All of our questions and doubts will not be answered in this life, but we will learn that we are a part of a real Person who loves us deeply. We will find, as Paul told the Athenians, "in him we live and move and have our being."(Acts 17:28)

KEEP YOUR EYES ON THE GOAL

The cardiac rehab program I was in began with a half hour of education on various related topics, structure of the heart, the vascular system, diet, followup exercises, etc. In talking about these aspects of health one has to consider, the instructor expressed something of a universal truth. "The benefit has to outweigh the effort it takes." Life itself is an effort. We are taught various guiding principles in Scripture. Some are difficult even as the hard sayings of Jesus, to love our enemies and do good to those who hate us. None of this comes naturally to our fallen nature even as good health doesn't. It requires care of the gift of life God has given, physically and spiritually. It is far easier to be self indulgent. However, our eyes must be on a different goal, a greater goal, a life that honors our Lord and lasts forever. That is a goal, a benefit, that far out weighs the effort of seeking, and desiring a life lived by faith in Jesus Christ. He has made it possible for us by His sacrifice on Calvary. He has granted forgiveness, and provided righteousness and new life. Now we live that life always looking forward in the marvelous grace He has given.

DON'T LIVE IN FEAR

I mentioned yesterday about the lectures in my PT sessions on various aspects related to heart health. There was another universal truth (or at least it should be) that the nurse spoke about. When one speaks or reads about all the various things that can happen to parts of our incredibly complex human bodies, one can begin to worry and start looking for symptoms of this illness or that. Our minds can play havoc with our emotions. But, said our teacher, beyond taking reasonable actions in modifying our lifestyle for our good, we cannot live in fear. This is a truth that is found throughout the Scripture. Our Lord tells us continually not to worry or be anxious, and this includes our health. That doesn't mean that we will never get sick or have a serious illness, or even one that is terminal. We live in a broken world and things happen to us. But we also believe that nothing touches us that our Lord doesn't know or care about. He does not cause all that happens, but He cares about it and can work in it for our good. To spite all the miracles recorded, there were a number of illnesses in the New Testament that weren't healed. Paul, himself, reports that he had what he called "a thorn in his flesh". He prayed three times for the Lord to remove it, but He didn't. Rather God told Paul,"My grace is sufficient for you, for power is perfected in weakness." (2 Corinthians 12:9) This has been proven in the lives of so many Christians through all the centuries. We are called to be good stewards of all the gifts God provides, including our bodies, but we are not to fear. We live in trust that our God is sufficient for all times of life.

SAY "I LOVE YOU"

We have a habit in the family of saying "I love you" frequently - when we end a phone conversation; when we are going out the door; or just at occasional times during the day. It has become an important habit for us. We all need to hear it, wives from husbands and visa versa, children from parents, and parents for children. Even good friends can share this sentiment. It is not just a casual or empty remark. It is not an awkward, syrupy expression. It is a word of assurance that you are important to me, and I will try always to do what is for your good. Above all, we need to hear it from our Lord. He has said it to us in a myriad of ways. "I love you so much that I gave My only Son for you."(John 3:16) We can be strong and get through our days doing what has to be done, but we also need the assurance that someone is standing beside us, someone to whom we matter very much. Above all know that you matter to the Lord.

Trusting God No Matter What

What is happening? The reports say the Coved19 virus is spreading worldwide with an increasing death toll. World financial markets are responding with tremendous losses. An oil price war had started between OPEC and Russia. People are hoarding products. Extra measures are being taken to disinfect public areas. Restrictions...Quarantines... (You can add our current series of trials.) What is happening? Is this something like the Old Testament judgments that God brought when His people rejected Him? I don't know, and I would never label it as such. But do we believe that God is involved in the human life He created? Do we believe that God knows and cares about all that touches us? We say this often enough. So where are our eyes? On the world alone, or on the Lord who redeemed us? That doesn't mean that we don't take proper precautions for cleansing and providing the things we need. We should, but where do we place our trust? In a quick fix, a new vaccine, a financial rally, or in the gracious Lord who has shown His love for us in so many ways? We may get the virus. We may suffer financial loss because of it. We may suffer in other ways. That's not pleasant, but we must understand that trusting God is not an automatic Get Out Of Jail Free card. Remember the penitent thief I wrote about a few days ago. Trusting God is committing ourselves into His pure and unmixed love knowing that His will for us is always good. What is happening? I don't really know, but trusting in the One on that center cross we can be at peace.

Our Soul's Prosperity

The Apostle John had made a number of close friendships as he traveled and shared the Gospel after the resurrection of our Lord. And he, like Paul and Peter, wrote letters of encouragement and guidance to them. One of his little letters that we have in the New Testament as Third John is to a friend named Gaius. "The elder to the beloved Gaius, whom I love in truth. Beloved, I pray that in all respects you may prosper and be in good health, just as your soul prospers."(3John 1&2) Hear his prayer. He desires that this close friend prospers, having the material things needed for a comfortable life, and that he be in good health. These are certainly the things we desire and pray for. But John also adds "just as your soul prospers". This, in the way John is expressing it, is what is of first importance. It points back to Jesus' words in Matthew six where He was telling His people not to worry about the material needs of life. "... your heavenly Father knows that you need all these things. But seek first His kingdom and His righteousness, and all these things will be added to you."(Matthew 6:32&33) I think we have forgotten a bit of this truth in our current fear of the spreading virus. We, myself included, have become very oriented toward our material peace and prosperity. We don't want to be denied. Now I've said that we should take reasonable precautions, but have we neglected the One who is our ultimate source of protection and care? Our trust is not in the ones working to make a vaccine or in the ones who supply our stores with goods. Our hope, our trust, is in the One who made us for His good purpose and who holds our very breath in His hands. In Him our soul prospers, and all else falls into its proper place.

BLESSED WITH EVERY SPIRITUAL BLESSING

The first chapter of Paul's letter to the Ephesian church is a marvelous statement of God's grace in calling us into a relationship with Himself. "Blessed be the God and Father of our Lord Jesus Christ, who has blessed us with every spiritual blessing in the heavenly places in Christ,.. In Him we have redemption through His blood, the forgiveness of our trespasses, according to the riches of His grace which He lavished on us." (Ephesians 1:3,7&8) Unmerited, undeserved redemption through the blood of Jesus...complete forgiveness...blessed with every spiritual blessing...all lavished upon us. Read the whole chapter slowly and consider your own calling by God into our faith in Jesus Christ. If we truly take this seriously we are completely humbled by the depth of such love. We are thankful beyond measure for this grace. Our lives become ones of grateful service, not to earn this great salvation, but to share this greatest of all gift - the gift of life now and eternally. You have begun a new day. Whatever this day holds, live it in the joy of this amazing grace.

Mi Case Es Su Case

In Spanish there is a greeting of welcome when someone come to another's home. "Mi case es su case." My house is your house. In English we would say "come in, make yourself at home". We want people to feel comfortable, to feel as if they are a part of us, to feel like family in our home. That is not unlike the welcome our Lord extends to us. We were created for a relationship with Him. But we were outside of that relationship. Our sin estranged us from our God. He had to reach out to bring us back in. Paul writing to the Ephesians Christians said, "in Christ Jesus you who formerly were far off have been brought near by the blood of Christ."(Ephesians 2:13) Think of the real picture this paints for our lives. We were outside, wandering around, seeking satisfaction, seeking peace in a variety of places, but not finding any real lasting satisfaction. Jesus comes out with an extended hand to invite us into His home. We enter by way of the cross finding a satisfaction, a truth, a value we had never known before. We have come home. Paul wrote "you are no longer strangers and aliens, but you are fellow citizens with the saints, and are of God's household..."(Ephesians 2:19) Think about that. In Christ Jesus we have come into our Father house and He says to us "mi case is su case".

Good Holy Fun With God

God is fun! That may seem like a strange thing to say. Too often we think of God as stern, or as awesome, or one to whom we have a duty to worship. These are true, but there is also great joy and holy fun in a relationship with the Lord. When God made man and woman He put them in a garden. He gave them the best of the best. Sin messed that up, but God still wants our best. God doesn't patronize us giving us everything we want, but He does lead us toward the best life possible. The best life is not like medicine. It tastes terrible, but it's good for you. A relationship with the Lord is joyful. The Bible says God laughs - especially at the silliness of His kids. Jesus had the most serious task in history, but I believe He laughed, too. He loved kids, and kids are funny. He loved fellowship and found great joy in companionship. To know God is the best joy possible. In Him we have good holy fun.

Know Where the Pot Holes Are

When we travel ten or more miles from home we usually take the same roads to the west or south. In a short while we learn where the pot holes and rough patches of paving are on those roads, and we avoid them. Thinking about this, it is not unlike the roads we travel in life. It doesn't take long to learn what things are the most temptations we face. They are the rough patches we need to avoid. It is like the saying, if you want to lose weight, don't go in a donut shop. The difference between the pot holes and the temptations is that what tempts us is something we really like. Even so, if we are seeking to live a life that honors our Lord, we try to avoid them. There is another difference. The pot hole is unforgiving and can lead to car repairs. In life, God's mercy is very great. When we fail in resisting our temptations, and come to the Lord in repentance, He does forgive and give us a new start. There really are many lessons on our road of life.

Stubborn Christians

Christians are to be stubborn. I been accused of that a time or two. But the issue is really the question of what we stubbornly stand for. If it is a matter of personal pride, or wanting to get one's way, that is one thing. That is self-centered and not good. On the other side, Paul writing to the Thessalonians says, "He called you to this through our gospel, that you might share in the glory of our Lord Jesus Christ. So then, brothers, stand firm and hold to the teachings we passed on to you,..."(2 Thesslonians 2:14-15) This is where stubbornness has its rightful and necessary place. We have been called by the Gospel. That is, by God grace through the Holy Spirit, we have heard and believed the truth of God's love for us in Jesus Christ. We have been given salvation and life through faith in Him. Through preaching, and teaching of the Holy Scriptures we have learned truths about who God is and the life He wants for us. It is upon these that we stand firm without compromise in those things that we know to be true. It is not easy in our secular world, but we have learned that it is only in our Lord that we have true life. We will stubbornly hold to it.

TRUE FREEDOM

On Independence Day in U.S. we celebrate the freedoms we enjoy that has been hard won for us over the past two and a quarter centuries. We rejoice in these freedoms and continually work to maintain them. But there is another kind of freedom that that is even more important. Jesus, in a discussion with the Pharisees, said "If you continue in My word, then you are truly disciples of Mine; and you will know the truth, and the truth will make you free."(John 8:31) The Jewish leaders argued with Him saying they had never been slaves to anyone. "Jesus answered them, 'Truly, truly, I say to you, everyone who commits sin is the slave of sin.'" (John8:34) There's that word again, "sin". It's the word we don't like and do everything possible to get around. Yet it is very real. It is anything that takes us away from the good life that God designed for mankind. But the sin that enslaves us is the very reason God provided the atoning sacrifice of Jesus Christ on the cross. The cross of Christ is the greatest symbol of our true freedom. We will do all we can to maintain our political freedom, but we live our lives in the truth that "if the Son makes you free, you will be free indeed."(John8:.36)

True Freedom - Continued

It is interesting when you look at freedom in the Bible. Personal freedom was not a great concern. Of course the Jews didn't like living under the thumb of Rome. But when Jesus came it was not His intent to change that. Even slavery was not prohibited, though Christian masters were taught not to treat their salves harshly. If a slave could gain his freedom, fine. If not, then serve in best efforts they could give. Certainly the kind of slavery we are familiar with is wrong, but personal liberty was not a central issue in Scripture. True freedom was found in a relationship with the Lord. Each of the Apostles called themselves the slaves of Christ. It was in a deep and personal relationship with the Lord Jesus that they found their true freedom. They were free from fear. They could be content in whatever circumstances they found themselves. They were willing to serve and give of themselves without worry about the future. They knew they were held in a love that would never leave them. They had no fear of death for they knew that they had already died and that their life was hidden with Christ in God. (Colossias 3:3) The same has been true for Christians through all the centuries since, and it is true today. We enjoy our personal freedoms, but our true freedom is found in the Lord Jesus Christ.

INCLUDE THE SCRIPTURES

In college classes various books are assigned. It is not uncommon for a professor to expect a number of chapters to be digested in a day or two. We manage to do it. We put in the time it takes. We want to understand the material and get the grade in the class. We've all done it, even though we may be well past that routine. Our academic and even entertainment reading is good, but it also must be balanced with the Scripture. With everything else we have to do we sometimes find it hard to give time to God's word. Besides, He isn't standing over us like a college professor. Yet it is only Scripture that balances all else that we read. It is only Scripture that corrects the errors we read elsewhere. Books can be very helpful, but only one book is the guide for discerning truth and error in all the rest. Solomon had access to all that the world had to give, yet he found only one source of true wisdom. "The words of the wise are like goads, their collected sayings like firmly embedded nails-given by one Shepherd." (Ecclesiastes 12:11) The words of our Lord are those "firmly embedded nails".

BEAUTY BEYOND MEASURE

At a recent worship service the Pastor had us sing the Lord's Prayer rather than say it as we usually do. There are a couple of different musical settings written, but we used the traditional and most familiar one. I have always found this a glorious and worshipful experience. I've done it alone by myself a time or two. Emotional? Yes, but the Lord created us as emotional beings. Our emotions are not to rule over the truth of God's Word, or the good judgment He give us. We have seen this cause havoc in too many situations. But when we are singing the Lord's own words, words He taught us to use in prayer, it becomes a real avenue of worship. There are many passages of Scripture that have been set to music. There are numerous times in the Bible where individuals respond to the Lord in song. Miriam, Hanna, Zachariah, Mary, Moses, and more. Something of the heart is poured out to our gracious Lord, and that is a beauty beyond measure.

PLAY BY THE DESIGNER'S RULES

I sometimes play Solitaire on my laptop computer. If I win a game the program has a display of fireworks that flashes up as it gives the final score. My young grandson likes to sit on my lap when I start playing. He's waiting to see the fireworks. He want to get his hands on the keyboard. I've tried to show him that a red card has to go on a black and numbers have to be in sequence. It takes some patience, understanding of the rules of the game, and often learning from the errors. But he wants to just punch the buttons and get to the fireworks. He will push my hand out of the way when I try to guide him. How about that as a lesson for life! Don't we do that, and watch it being done, in many areas of life? We just want to push a few buttons and get to the fireworks without all the patience, studying to understand the rules, and learning from our mistakes. This is especially true in the sexual aspects of life. A designer created the game of Solitaire, and it need to be played by his rules. Life also has a Designer and has established the way in which it is to be played. We get to the fireworks when we play be the rules. *(There is more to be said about the game of life and its Designer, but we will get to that tomorrow.)*

MORE THAN A PLAY OVER OPTION

In my computer Solitaire game there is a button at the top of the screen where I can replay the same deal over. If I play a set and don't win, I can play the same hand over again and try to correct my mistakes. The rules don't change, but I am allowed to try a different path. Yesterday I likened the rules of the game to the way of life our Lord has established for our good. And we lose when we don't follow them. But our gracious Lord is far better than the play over option on my computer game. We do mess up in His rules for life, but He has provided the way for forgiveness, cleansing, and a new life. In Jesus Christ we receive not just a new deal with the same old cards, but an entirely new life. About our baptism into Christ, the Apostle Paul says that we have died with Him. The old life is buried with Him, and we are raised to a new life lived in the resurrected Lord Jesus. (Romans 6) We still sin because we are in this fallen nature, but sin is not who we are. In Christ we have a new identity. We are assured that there is "no condemnation for those who are in Christ Jesus". (Romans 8:1) That is far better than a do over in my Solitaire game.

A Servant Ruler

In Deuteronomy 17 there is a very interesting set of instructions for kings. I think we could also say they are good for all rulers. They were told first to be of the people, and not a foreigner. He was not to acquire many horses for himself, not to return to Egypt, not to take many wives, not to acquire large amounts of silver and gold, and to read the book of God's law each day. Let's bring these symbols up into our modern context. We would say that a ruler must be one of us. That is to understand us and our needs. He is not to seek great strength and power for himself - dare we say even forgetting political consideration for the next election in order to do what is right. He is not to return to the pagan ways of the world and its idolatry. He is to be faithful to his marriage covenant. He is not to seek office for material gain. And he is to read the Scriptures seeking God's wisdom daily. It seems to me that these are good instructions for a leader in any age. But then I guess I'm expecting too much in our modern world.

GOOD MORNING SAINTS

Good morning saints. In Paul's letters he frequently refers to the people in the churches he established as saints. What is striking is that many of them were not "acting" saintly as we might think of it. Particularly with Corinth and Galatia he had to speak pretty harshly to them. Yet he called them saints. Of course he wants them to live holy lives, but what he is continually pointing to is the work God was doing in them, and not what they merit personally. He is clear in writing to the Philippians saying "it is God who works in you to will and to act in order to fulfill his good purpose. (Philiippians 2:13) He tells the Colossian church that it is He who "has rescued us from the dominion of darkness and brought us into the kingdom of the Son he loves, in whom we have redemption, the forgiveness of sins." (Philippians1:13-14) No, we don't feel like saints, and a lot of times we don't act like saints, yet God declares that is who we truly are through faith in Jesus Christ. He sees the end from the beginning, and Paul has given us the promise that "He who began a good work in you will carry it on to completion until the day of Christ Jesus." (Philippians 1:6) So I say again, good morning saints.

Add The Nation To Your Prayer List

We are familiar with intercessory prayer. Many of us use a daily prayer lists, praying for friend's and relative's needs. There is another aspect of prayer we need to make more intentional. It is called standing in the gap. There were a number of times God was angry with Israel on their journey out of Egypt. He was ready to destroy the nation until Moses pleaded with the Lord on their behalf, staying God's hand of judgment. The Apostle Paul pleaded with God on behalf of his people, the Jewish nation. At a late time in Israel's history God said to the Prophet Ezekiel, "I looked for a man among them who would build up the wall and stand before me in the gap on behalf of the land so I would not have to destroy it, but I found none." (Ezekiel 22:31) We rightly pray for the needs of those we know, but we need to cry out more and more to our Lord for mercy on behalf of our nation and all of this broken world. Diplomats and legislators will not solve our problems. We need God's presence, mercy, and grace. Stand in the gap for all of our people.

TODAY IS A DAY OF GRACE

Most people know what TGIF means. (Thank God it's Friday) When it comes to the first day of the work week many begin with OGIM. And with the virus threat we now face its possible to feel that way about every day. But that's really not the way to begin. Each day is a day of grace, even in the midst of a storm. Each day God opens new opportunities, new things to learn and enjoy. Certainly, we may not look forward to particular tasks of the day or the fears we face with the choices confronting us, but even these are not apart from our Lord. We are the clay. He is the Potter. He uses everything to shape us into a useful and good vessel. Did you ever watch a potter, or perhaps a glass blower? The craftsman uses heat, pressure, and various instruments to shape the mass of material. It is exciting to see a beautiful object emerge. You are that beautiful object as you yield to Him in trust and hope. Can we see the challenges and choices we currently face as God's gracious hand working to shape us, to open our hearts more to Him? Our gracious Lord will continue to work in each of our days until that work is complete.(Philippians 1:6) Even on this Friday the 13th which is supposed to be unlucky. So it's not OGIM, but TYLFTGOTD. Thank you Lord for the grace of this day.

STRENGTH NOT IN OURSELVES

I love St. Peter. He has a strong character. He is not afraid. He is the first one to step up and declare his loyalty to the Lord. "I will lay down my life for you Lord."(John 13: 37) Yet Jesus had to say to him, "Will you lay down your life for Me? Truly, truly, I say to you, a rooster will not crow until you deny Me three times." Within not too many hours of Peter's declaration of loyalty he was in the courtyard of the High Priest waiting to see what would happen to Jesus after He was arrested. Confronted by a servant girl and two others Peter denied even knowing Jesus. I can't imagine what Peter felt when he heard that rooster crow. He was crushed. He had denied the One he said he loved. He denied the One with whom he had spent the last three years in close fellowship. He had denied the One who had sent him on missions with the power to heal and cast out demons. He had denied Him, and he was crushed. But it had to happen. It has to happen to all of us. After Jesus's resurrection, in His marvelous grace, He restored Peter to fellowship. But Peter's fall was necessary. It took his eyes off of himself, his strength, his abilities, and focused them on the only One who could truly give him strength and guide his abilities. In whatever time or situation we find ourselves, where are our eyes? In whom is our confidence? We use the gifts we've been given, but our strength is only in Jesus.

OUR BIG GOD

I've said before, God boggles my mind! I cannot fathom the magnitude of our Lord and His Kingdom. But then I'm not supposed to. If God were no bigger than my mind He wouldn't be a God worth believing in. We do get glimpses into His life. Looking into the visible cosmos with all its immense size, and beauty leaves us enthralled with its grandeur. Yet even this is but a small part of God's creation. The second chapter of Paul's letter to the Colossians speaks of "a true knowledge of God's mystery, and all the treasures of wisdom and knowledge."(Colossians 2:2-3) Paul makes it clear that all of this is centered in the person of Jesus Christ. As Paul has said in the first chapter "He is the image of the invisible God, the firstborn of all creation."(Colossians 1:15) The fulness of our Lord is truly incomprehensible. Yet He does want us to know Him. He has revealed Himself in the person of His son, Jesus Christ, and through Him we gain insight into mysteries of our God.

THE POWER OF SACRIFICE

Sacrifice, a word not held in high favor today, but one very necessary to consider. We certainly know the value of sacrifice in the Scriptures. Old Testament sacrifices, while seeming to be a bloody mess, were an act of obedience and faith for the people. They were also an important lesson pointing forward to the New Testament ultimate sacrifice in Jesus Christ. The sacrifice of Christ is the means of life for us all. We share in that sacrificial death and Jesus' resurrection from the dead through our baptism.[Romans 6] Now the life of that great sacrificial love becomes our model. We sacrifice when we willingly put another's interest ahead of our own, when we hold our tongue instead of biting back, when we suffer some injustice instead of demanding our rights. Good relationships are built on sacrifice. The central question is what I can give, not what I can get. Maybe, if we are willing to think further in the context of our society, we sacrifice some portion of our government entitlements, or set aside political considerations in favor of the common good, we will find a better life together. We have been given the greatest life possible through the sacrifice of Jesus Christ. Young and old alike need to seriously think what sacrifice means for daily life.

THE NAME OF JESUS

When some Christians talk about their spiritual life in a group of people, especially if some of them are unfamiliar to the speaker, they are sometimes reluctant to mention the name of Jesus. After all, the name of Jesus can be divisive and we don't want to offend people. Well, it is true that Jesus can divide people. He said of Himself "Do you suppose that I came to grant peace on earth? I tell you, no, but rather division;..."(Luke 12:51) Jesus said, "I am the way and the truth and the life. No one comes to the Father except through me."(John 14:6) There are not many truths or many ways. The Apostle Peter would later make a defense before the Jewish authorities by saying, "Salvation is found in no one else, for there is no other name under heaven given to mankind by which we must be saved."(Acts 4:12) Now, I'm not one for "in your face evangelism". That can turn more people off than bring them to the Lord. Even so we cannot hide the name of Jesus. If we call ourselves Christians that means ones who follow the Christ. He is the One who has loved us so deeply that He gave His life so that we might live. We do not force anyone to believe, but we do seek to live in the love of Christ, and to share with people that our joy is in Him alone.

Within God's Structure

There have been celebrations recently of the 50th anniversary of the massive Woodstock rock concert that took place on a farm in New York. Bands from all over the country came to play for a group estimated at half a million teenage and twenty something people. One of those musicians was a young man named Carlos Santana. He later remarked that "What I learned most from Woodstock is that people are thirsty to live, to exist outside of religion and politics." Things have changed a lot in 50 years, but I don't think Santana is too far wrong about the basic nature of many people. Religion, they feel, puts too many restrictions on life. It causes an internal battle with the "I want" versus what they perceive God (however they conceive of him) wants. That's right back to the first temptation in the Garden. And politics (while I dislike much about politics myself) does seek to provide a structure for the good of society. Yet our good and gracious Lord calls us to live within a structure that is for our best good. It is He who created us and knows us to the core of our being. We are called and invited to come to Him, finding in Him our way of life. Even when that means giving up our own will.

The Man Upstairs?

A neighbor up the street was seriously ill some time ago. In talking with him after his recovery he credited "the Man upstairs" for helping him through. It's not an uncommon phrase. I expect we have all heard the Lord referred to in that way. This same man has spoken at times about difficulties and strife at home. Somehow "the Man upstairs" doesn't fit into that for him. It seems to me that the Man upstairs is a distant God, unconcerned about smaller everyday aspects of life. He is the God we look to in dire need, but otherwise don't see Him involved with life. This is not the God who has revealed Himself to us in Holy Scripture. The God who willingly left Glory to live 33 years in human flesh, to experience all that we face in life, to give Himself in atonement for all of our sins, and to be raised again from the dead giving us the assurance of life eternal. We worship the living God who knows every sparrow, and can even care about a lost set of car keys, as I've heard one of our parishioner say. Our Lord is not a distant God, but one who cares about, and is involved with all life.

YET WILL I TRUST HIM!

We've experienced unusual and fearful times. We are seeing a new virus spread worldwide at a rate none of us have experienced before. We see an abundance of storms and tornadoes. Heat waves in triple digits. Wars and rumors of wars. Political chaos. What to do? How do we respond? We are taking as many health precautions as we can. We are trying to provide support, financial and otherwise, for those in need. Yes, it is a fearful and uncertain time. On the night before Jesus' arrest, the Apostles were facing such a time. They didn't know what was ahead, and a deep foreboding pervaded each heart. It was then Jesus said to them,"Peace I leave with you; My peace I give to you; not as the world gives do I give to you. Do not let your heart be troubled, nor let it be fearful."(John 14:27) His words add a whole different perspective to what we face. We are not lax in doing all that is prudent and necessary. We do not "put God to the test" demanding He take care of us. But the assurance we have here from Jesus, is that all things are ultimately in our Lord's hands. He is good. He will bring all things to their right conclusion. We really dislike not knowing what is ahead. We don't like feeling out of control. But we can trust our Lord. Even as Job said, who knew more than his share of trouble, "Though he slay me, yet will I trust in him..."(Job 13:15) Even if we don't know what is ahead, Jesus is our peace.

ABIDE

My morning reading included John chapter 15, The Vine and The Branches. It speaks of our need to "abide" in Jesus in order to accomplish what is good and God-glorifying - "bearing fruit". I've pondered that word "abide" off and on for years. In a quick reading we could say it means to believe in Jesus as God's Son and our Lord. True, but I've always thought it was much deeper than that. I really can't give you a good answer, but there is something deep and meaningful to which we are being invited by our Lord. I've also read recently the text in First Samuel 18 about the bond that Jonathan, King Saul's son, had with David. "He loved him like his own soul." It seems that this may approach an understanding of the depth of that word abide. It is in this very real relationship with our Saviour that we have a depth of confidence, joy, and peace no matter the outward situation. I would think that pondering, and growing in "abiding" in Jesus, the true vine, is what we need in this uncertain time. It is what I need. There is no guarantee against sickness, suffering, and death, but there is a guarantee that "nothing is able to separate us from the love of God which is in Christ Jesus our Lord". (Romans 8:39) In that we have strength for all times and needs.

All Is A Gift From God

As a young child going to church with my parents, when time came for the offering plate to be passed, my Mom would give me a quarter to put in the plate myself. I expect some of you experienced the same thing. It was my money for a short time, but it really wasn't mine. It had been given me in order to give away for a greater purpose. That's how God, our Father treats us. All that we have, our talents, abilities, intelligence, personality, physical strength, and material possessions, have been given to us. We can't call them our own. We are entrusted with them for a time to use for a greater good, for God, and for God's people. Sometimes, we would have rather kept that quarter for our own use. And certainly a part of what we have is for our own care and that of our family. But whether we realized it or not, with that first quarter we were learning a truth about our life. To squander or fail to give back what we have been given, benefits no one, and we ultimately hurt ourselves. What we have is a gift from God and to be used for our good and the good of others.

Just a Mustard Seed

Small things are important. A woman came to Jesus asking for healing for her daughter. Her faith was such that she said she only needed a crumb size blessing from God and her daughter would be healed. Another time Jesus commended a poor widow for putting just two pennies in the offering box. And still another time He said that we only need faith the size of a tiny mustard seed to be able to do great things. In our bigger is better world, Jesus calls us to be faithful in the small things. We don't need to yearn for more, or wish we could be better at something. We simply recognize that all we have is His. He gave it to us and we seek to use everything to honor Him. Jesus' greatest example of faith, the faith that inherits the Kingdom, was a little child set in their midst. We take care of the small things, and God will see to the big ones.

Worldly Promises Found Lacking

Some time back a local merchant sent out prize certificates to the community as part of an advertising campaign. You know the kind. Scratch off the silver coating, and see if your number matches the winning number. Well, ours did. We won a thousand dollar shopping spree. Pretty good, right? All the shopping was to be done at an online site. The things offered were small and generally not very useful. Even further, we would have to pay the shipping cost, which amounted to about half the price of the item. The promises on the outside were not matched by what was available on the inside. Such is never the case with our Lord. Jesus said, "I have come that you may have life, and have it more abundantly." (John 10:10) God doesn't give us everything we want in life. At times we have to endure pain and suffering. But the promise of His eternal presence is always true. The deeper we go in the life our Lord provides, the richer that life becomes. We learn that His strength and grace are better than any worldly prizes. His promises are never hollow, or lacking. The promises of this life often let us down. God's never will. And the best is yet to come.

A Work In Progress

I love to sing, and when I can stay on tune (which does happen occasionally) I can do a fairly good job of it. I grew up with a lot of old Gospel songs. I still love them. Of course, we sing a lot of hymns in church. But I've become more and more aware of the words I'm singing. These are statements I am saying. Do I really mean them? "Take my life and let it be consecrated Lord to Thee ... Take my silver and my gold. Not a mite would I withhold." I'm not sure that's really true. I am concerned about my worldly possessions. And there are many others, too. We can get caught up in a great melody, but we need to think about the words. What it points out to me is what Martin Luther wrote many years ago. We are at the same time saint and sinner. As long as we are in this flesh this is the struggle we face. But it also says that we are works in progress. The fact that we are willing to ask a question about the words we sing says that God isn't finished with us yet. I will continue to sing with great thanksgiving for the grace and mercy of our Lord who is working to bring us to Himself.

BEAUTY IN THE DEFECT

When one is getting out a piece of wood for a woodworking project, there are times when that slab will still have some tree bark adhering to the side. On others there may be a knot hole, or a crack in one place or another. These look like defects in the board and make one think the board should be discarded. I was sitting in a doctors office recently waiting for my wife. Next to me was a small wood occasional table made out of a two inch thick slab of oak. The top was smooth, but the edge had a long irregular bark filled notch in the side. The table was finished and polished and absolutely beautiful. What appeared originally as a defect to be discarded was the very thing that gave the piece its beauty and character. Quite a lesson really when we think about the people we see in life. Ones who are handicapped, mentally challenged, or otherwise considered "defective" are the very ones who can bring joy and meaning to life. It is these that Jesus sought out, spent time with, and at time considered far better than the "good" people who surrounded Him. There are lots of lessons in many of the small things of life. Keep looking.

TRUST IN WHOM?

There are numerous passages of Scripture saying how God does not look on things as man does, but He looks at the individual heart. Beyond the need for proper care and following recommendations to stop the spread of the Coronavirus, what is this massive worldwide outbreak saying? I was in our local supermarket a day or two ago. You've likely been there, also. Many shelves, even of nonessentials, were bare. I talked to one of the stock clerks asking if they were having trouble getting things from their suppliers. He said, "Not so much. It was just that people were hoarding so many things". People were going to the Checkout with 10s and 20s of the same item. (The store is now limiting customers to two items.) This points out something important, and this is the spiritual component to our present situation. The current pandemic is showing something of what is inside of us. We say that our Lord is involved in all of life in this world He created. He is not unaware or uncaring about what we go through. Is He using this time to help us see more clearly something of our own nature, and calling us to put more of our trust in Him? Along with our hand cleanser, perhaps we should pray a prayer of repentance for ourselves and our people, and ask His help to trust Him more.

IN THE POTTER'S HANDS

I've always loved the image of the potter and the clay the Lord used with the Prophet Jeremiah.[(18:1)] I used this a few days ago in one of my messages. There is also a song we occasionally sing, Have Thine Own Way Lord. One of its lines says "Thou art the Potter, I am the clay." That song is part of the reason Audrey and I left a career in Engineering and went into the Ministry. As time has gone on for more than 50 years our Lord has been so very gracious. Not all of those years have been easy. And I can't say that I like all the things we face today. I've always pondered what that lump of clay felt as it spun on the Potter's wheel with the Potter's thumbs pressing in its sides! Personifying that clay, it can't feel very good. But like the line in the song says, we are that clay. The question we now face in the midst of all the restrictions, changes, and sacrifices we have to make because of restrictions placed on us - Do we want to just go back to being the lump of clay with everything just as it was before? Or do we want to yield to the Potter's hands honestly seeking to hear what He is saying to us in this time? Business as usual, or perhaps a complete change in life's direction? Our gracious God is never far off, and He is not silent. It is for us to become quiet in heart before Him and listen.

LOVED WITH SCARS

Throughout the Christian centuries people who have understood the depth of love God has for them have been willing to sacrifice their own time and well being for the good of others, even to hold their convictions to the point of martyrdom. It is the knowledge that we are loved with the everlasting love of God that causes us to be willing to do everything necessary to remain in that love. But there is another sense in which there is nothing we can do, good or bad, to get out of His love. That doesn't mean we can do whatever we please and it doesn't matter. Of course, what we do matters, but I think of the parable of the Prodigal Son in Luke 15. The son's rebellion was terrible, even wishing his father dead by asking for his inheritance. Yet the father's love for the wayward son never ceased. The father was on the porch of the family home day by day praying for his son, looking down the farm lane, and longing for him to come to his senses. The son, you and I, separate ourselves from that love by our sins. We suffer the consequences of our actions, but we can't stop the Father from loving us. "Because Jesus lives forever, he has a permanent priesthood. Therefore he is able to save completely those who come to God through him, because he always lives to intercede for them." [Hebrews 7:24-25] Jesus is praying for us that we remain strong, and always know the depth of His love.

With Eyes On Jesus

Where are our eyes? There is an account in Matthew 14 where Jesus, walking on the water, comes to the disciples on the storm tossed Galilean lake. He called to His men who were struggling and afraid in the fishing boat. The text says that Peter got out of the boat and began to walk toward the Lord on the water. (Matthew 14:29) When Jesus invited Peter to come to Him, He didn't first still the storm. In the midst of the storm He simply said, "Come". As long as Peter's eyes were on Jesus he continued to walk forward. When his eyes fell from Jesus to the raging sea he began to sink. We face many storms in life, and they just don't go away. That's the nature of our fallen world. Writing to the Corinthians, Paul tells of a serious problem he had. He writes, "Three times I pleaded with the Lord to take it away from me. But he said to me, "My grace is sufficient for you, for my power is made perfect in weakness."(II Corinthians 12:8-9) Paul found that strength, as did Peter, because their eyes were on the Lord Jesus. No part of life is ever going to be exactly the way we want it. Yet, our strength is not in the smooth going, it is in our Lord who walks with us whether the seas are stormy or calm. That's where our eyes need to be.

THE GOOD OLD DAYS?

A couple of mailings I received in the last two days are interesting. A magazine cover has a picture of an old mill, a water race and stream. Obviously a mill active a century or more ago. A mailing from a charity had a calendar with picture of farm and home life in the late 19th and early 20th centuries. I've remarked before about people's desire for antiques. A small town near us was know as the Antique Capital of Maryland. The pictures are beautiful, and I've enjoyed working with a number of antique pieces, but I wonder if there isn't something deeper that this is saying. Are people longing for a simpler, less complicated time. No time in history after the Fall has been ideal but we've grown into such a fast, paced, complex lifestyle that we are under a great deal of pressure just to get through our days. I was talking to a man last evening who has an hour and a half commute to work daily. I spent two hours today trying to get a computer problem solved, with all of its attending frustration. We struggle to find a level of calmness and peace in life. Yet Jesus still stands in the midst of us with His invitation to "Come unto me, all ye that labor and are heavy laden, and I will give you rest." (Matthew 11:18) We will still struggle to find ways to simplify our lives, but the invitation is always there, and it is real.

Our Rock

Sometimes when reading the Bible one or two verses will stand out as very meaningful for that day or situation. Most everyone know the opening of Psalm 23, "The Lord is my Shepherd I shall not want." I have one for you for today. Here are the first three verses of Psalm 18. "I love You, O LORD, my strength. The LORD is my rock and my fortress and my deliverer, My God, my rock, in whom I take refuge; My shield and the horn of my salvation, my stronghold. I call upon the LORD, who is worthy to be praised, And I am saved from my enemies." Think about that. This is the Lord, your God and my God. He is the love of our life, the rock on which we stand. We face enemies in this day, even if it is just the time pressure to get everything done. He is our stronghold in the midst of all life, and most worthy to be praised. Let this be your verse for today, and perhaps many days. This is the Lord who is near at hand, and in whose love we rest.

MY RIGHT OR GOD'S GRACE?

I correspond with a pastor friend of mine in Tanzania east African. In fact I will be visiting there in the middle of next month. It is very interesting to hear of his ministry and the conditions under which he works. "Interesting" is really not a good word. It sounds like I can stand aloof and pity him. Rather, I do appreciate him for his dedication to the Gospel, and willingness to carry it forward, even under very difficult circumstances. I'm not sure I would be able to do it. Then too, sharing with these African friends helps me to look at my own life in a different light. I try not to take anything for granted, as my right, or something that I deserve. Whatever I have is by the grace of God, and I am reminded of Jesus words, "to whom much is given, much is required." (Luke 12:48) Whether in Africa, or in the U.S., we are stewards of God's gracious gifts, to use them wisely and to His glory.

One Account, One Purpose, One Love

Many Christians read the Bible regularly. Many others have at least some familiarity it. But the whole Bible, Old and New Testaments, only makes sense when seen from its central figure, Jesus of Nazareth. Jesus only make sense when understood from who He is, the Son of God in human flesh. And God becoming incarnate in Jesus can only be understood by seeing the reason for which He came. We were separated from God by our sin, by our rebellion from His will. He had created us to be in fellowship with Him, but we had separated ourselves and there was nothing we could do to restore that fellowship. God had to do it by taking the just punishment we deserve into Himself, making atonement for our sins. That is what the cross is all about. So when we read the Bible the cross of Jesus Christ casts a long shadow over every page bringing it together as one book showing the depth of love God has for mankind to bring us back into fellowship with Himself.

Just Turn Around

There was a good comment in a monthly newsletter I received from our local Rescue Mission. The director wrote "You may move 10,000 steps away from God, but if you turn around He is only one step behind." This is something of a paraphrase of St. John's words, "If we confess our sins He is faithful and just to forgive our sins and cleanse us from all unrighteousness". (1John1:9) This is no license to live in any way we please and then expect God to forgive and accept us. But it is the assurance that no sin is unforgivable, and if we honestly repent (turn around) He does cleanse and renew our lives. The Rescue Mission has proven this many times over, but it is a truth we each depend upon for the daily renewal of our lives.

OUR TRUST IN AN IMPERFECT WORLD

This is not a perfect world. Nor are the things in our personal lives perfect. Our jobs don't always go the way we would like. Kids don't always behave. Things get put away in the wrong places. Computers crash, and you can add to the list of irritating imperfections. The problem is we want things to be perfect. We don't want to deal with the irritations. It's frustrating. It makes us angry. But it is what it is, and our irritated attitude is not going to make things better. The only way to meet the imperfections of life is with a nature that is perfect. There is only one. Jesus. That may sound simplistic, but we are called to look to Him, to trust Him, to seek our strength in Him for all our times of life. He doesn't cause all the situations we face, but He can work in them and use them for our good. No one faced more trials than our Lord when He walked this earth in our human flesh. He met these trials with His nature of "love, joy, peace, forbearance, kindness, goodness, faithfulness, gentleness and self-control." (Galatians 5:22-23) That is what God's spirit is continually seeking to work in our lives. Of course, we don't live in these attributes perfectly, but think about it. If we were to meet the trials of life with more of these perfect characteristics, they would have a real power to change the present situations into something just a bit more perfect. Day by day we seek to yield in trust to the Hands that are shaping us.

Learn To Be Quiet

In the busyness of our world we need t learn how to be quiet. It is not easy, but if we lose our ability to be quiet and think, we also lose our ability to draw near to our Lord and find our strength in Him. God is not just out there somewhere, a power we call on occasionally when we are in need. God is a rational person who desires that we learn to know Him. When Paul was speaking to the philosophers in Athens, he said that God created mankind "so that they would seek him and perhaps reach out for him and find him, though he is not far from any one of us."(Acts 17:27) This is an amazing truth that is stated throughout our Scriptures. Our sins have made a separation between us, but that has not changed God's desire for us to know and draw near to Him. He has perfectly revealed Himself to us in Jesus Christ, who once said to Philip, "anyone who has seen me has seen the Father."(John 14:9) God has come to us in Jesus. He has done everything necessary for us to know and have a relationship with Him, but He will not force Himself on us. He invites us to come, to read His Word, to become quiet before Him, to think, and to pray. All of our questions and doubts will not be answered in this life, but we will learn that we are a part of a real Person who loves us deeply. We will find, as Paul told the Athenians, "in him we live and move and have our being."(Acts17:28)

Wherever We Are

Where can I go from you Spirit? Where can I flee from you presence? If I go up to the heavens, you are there; if I make my bed in the depths, you are there. If I rise on the wings of the dawn, if I settle on the far side of the sea, even there your hand will guide me, your right hand will hold me fast." [Psalm 139:7-10] Each of us is a creation of God. He gives us life and breath. As the Psalmist says, He follows us wherever we are. He has been called the Hound of Heaven. It is the awesome mystery of His love that causes Him to continue to seek us, and want to work in our life. Whether we know it or not, His right hand is upon us today.

The Lord Is My Shepherd

Psalm 23 came up this morning as part of my daily reading. This "shepherd's psalm" is the best loved of all the Psalms. It is the one that families have asked to be read at almost all the funerals I've had. Yet it is really a psalm for life. Psalm 95 tells us "For he is our God; and we are the people of his pasture, and the sheep of his hand."(Psalm 23:7) The Shepherd uses the rod of guidance and correction, and the staff of protection and restoration each day to bring us to good pastures and still waters. The images are rather foreign to us, but their truth remains. We do face our valleys of the shadow of death in a variety of trials, but the Lord is still there. His word to us continually is do not fear, do not be anxious. He can be trusted for all we face in each day. His goodness and mercy does follow us, and we have the assurance that we dwell in His house now and forever. Far from being a funeral psalm, these are truths we rest upon daily.

RECYCLED

Recycling is big today. Everyone recognizes that we make too much trash and need to reuse a lot of our throwaway material. I put my big blue container out by the street with it's two weeks worth of newspapers, plastic containers, glass jars, and cans. Then tomorrow when I go to buy a ream of copy paper it will have been made from some of those same recycled materials. Obviously, recycling is a good idea. If you think about it, God is first one who declared recycling a good idea. In His grace He has been recycling people since the Fall. Man's nature is self-willed and opposed to God. Over the years of life we make wrong decisions separating ourselves from our Lord. But God is not willing to throw us away. We have His forgiving grace through Jesus Christ who is "the atoning sacrifice for our sins, and not only for ours but also for the sins of the whole world". [I John 2:2] He continually reaches out, seeking to get us to turn in faith to Him. He extends His sure promise, "If we confess our sins, He is faithful and just to forgive our sins and cleanse us from all unrighteousness." [I John 1:9] There is no better recycling than this. In Christ "the old things passed away; behold, new things have come." [II Corinthians 5:17] Think about that the next time you put that blue container by the road.

Be The Salt

John Kennedy, in his presidential inaugural address, had his famous line , "Ask not what your country can do for you, but what you can do for your country". It is actually an important admonition for many areas of life. It is striving to think beyond ourselves for what we can accomplish for others. Paul had a concern for the Corinthian church being too enamored with spiritual gifts in a self-centered way. He spends a whole chapter helping them see the need to edify the whole Christian body, and not just themselves. This is a word that applies in every area of life, family, work, charitable organizations, church, and even daily human interactions. What do we do, what do we bring, to each life situation that is even a small measure of edification. Jesus said "you are the salt of the earth...you are the light of the world". [Matthew 5:13-16] The amazing thing about seeking to live as salt and light is that it is where we find our greatest joy and fulfillment.

A Love So Great

Some years ago I went to a weekend men's retreat called Via De Christo. It is a structured time of reflection, renewal and personal growth. There were several presentations, small groups at round tables, and exercises to complete and discuss. One man had been invited who had no concept of why we were there, and was not all that pleased with the program. His comment, "I thought I was coming to hear some good preaching". His idea of "good preaching" was hell fire and damnation which either tore you apart, or more likely let you point your finger at those bad guys out there. That is certainly is not what this weekend was all about, and it really is not what "good preaching" is. We don't need to be frightened with the threat God's wrath, but rather humbled before the cross by a depth of love so great that it was willing to take all our sins into itself giving us the perfect gift of His righteousness before God. In the depth of such love hearts are changed and lives reborn.

CULTIVATION

Our local newspaper has an interesting or thought provoking quote on the front page each day. Last Friday's was by a Japanese farmer/philosopher by the name of Masanobu Fukuoka. He said that "the ultimate goal of farming is not the growing of crops, but the cultivation and perfection of human beings". There has always been an important connection between the land and the nature of people. Both created by God. We are supposed to learn from the things in nature that God created. Farming is hard work, but as Fukuoka said is has a way of cultivating and perfecting people. However, since the Industrial Revolution more and more of us have gotten away from the land. The family farm is far less common than it was years ago. We have become far more dependent upon the supermarket than we have the good earth of God's creation. Now I'm not going back to growing my own food anytime soon, but a thought like this helps us to understand the changes in the nature of our society over the past hundreds of years. And not all those changes have been good. It is one more factor contributing to our lack of closeness and understanding of our God who has made us and all things.

GIVING

The Bible speaks about tithing as the standard for giving to the Lord. The tithe is ten percent of one's income. Malachi 3:10 tells us, "Bring the whole tithe into the storehouse, ... and test Me now in this," says the LORD of hosts, "if I will not open for you the windows of heaven and pour out for you a blessing until it overflows." Now, God is not an accountant, and we are freed from the requirements of the Old Testament law. Nor do we have to dicker over whether that ten percent is of the net or gross. The issue is really a matter of trusting in the Lord. Do we believe that the Lord can provide for our needs? If you look at all you now have, whether little or great, as a gift from God, then you've already seen His provision for your life. Giving is a joy in sharing what He has provided, and not the burden of an obligation. If the decision is to give two or three percent, that's fine. As we try increasing our giving our faith also grows, and we have the joy of being a blessing to others.

HOLD FAST

In Deuteronomy, the fifth book of the Old Testament, Moses is giving final instruction to the people of Israel before they cross over the Jordan River and enter the Promised land. They are to keep themselves from sin and not take up any of the false and idolatrous practices of the pagan peoples. He writes, "It is the LORD your God you must follow, and him you must revere. Keep his commands and obey him; serve him and hold fast to him."(Deuteronomy13:4) The word "hold fast" is the same Hebrew word that is used in Genesis 2:24 for the relationship of a husband and wife. The King James version says that the man shall "cleave" to his wife and they become one. The word means to follow close, to be joined together, to cling. Moses was saying that we are to be joined together with our Lord in the same way as a husband and wife are joined together. They become one flesh. This has met many challenges in our modern era, but the instruction has not changed. For us to stay faithful to our Lord, to seek to live lives that honor Him and are a blessing to us, we continually seek to grow in our relationship to the Lord. Just as a husband cleaves, holds fast to His wife so we daily hold fast to our Lord.

What Is Truth?

In talking with some of His followers Jesus said, "If you hold to my teaching, ... you will know the truth, and the truth will set you free."(John 8:31-32) Later on at His trial before Pilate He said, "...the reason I was born and came into the world is to testify to the truth. Everyone on the side of truth listens to me." Yet Pilate asked "What is truth?"(John 18:37-38) Pilate's question seem to hang over our world. Truth today gets bent according to pre-established agendas. Real truth is set aside because it doesn't conform to the program one is fostering. "If you hold to my teaching" Jesus said, "you will know the truth." All truth, and I underline All, has its origin in God who created us and all that is. Whether science, or government, or affairs among people, all is guided and governed by the truth of God's word. We set that aside to our own peril. We have the challenge to search and understand what is in the Bible, God's Holy Word, and to seek to live it in the community where God has placed us. It is not always easy, but as Jesus said, in that is true freedom.

Dry Days

Good Morning dear friends. There are some days when I am running late, and some days when I'm dry without any thoughts or direction. Today is one of them. So I ask your pardon and indulgence. It is certainly not that our Lord is without thought or direction. Nor is He ever late. That is the Lord in whom we trust to see us through not only our dry days, but all days. He is able. So we will begin this day taking one step at a time, and doing the best we can with the task that comes next. God's blessings, strength, and guidance for your day.

Death Overcome

Facing the death of a loved one is a painful experience. There is no way to sugar coat it. The separation from a loved one is hard at any age, one of the most painful of life's experiences. Death is the result of sin that entered at the first rebellion of mankind from God and has corrupted the world ever since. But even at the time of that first rebellion God gave the promise of a Redeemer who would break the power of sin, death and the devil. It is by faith in that Redeemer, Jesus, the Christ, that we know - to use St. Paul's words "we are convinced" - that death as painful as it is, is temporary. Even as Jesus said to Martha "he who lives and believe in me will live even if he dies."(John 14:25) We still bear the pain of death, a reminder of the sin that so easily besets us, but we are comforted by the truth that even this great pain is not final, and we do rejoice in the truth that nothing, not even death, can separate us from the love of God in Christ Jesus our Lord.(Romans 8:39).

OUR STRENGTH

We put new a message up on our church sign. It was from the Old Testament book of Nehemiah chapter 8 verse 10. Some of the Israelites had returned from exile in Babylon. They had started rebuilding the Temple, but it was a poor picture of the former Temple that had been destroyed by the Babylonians because of Israel's rebellion. On this day of dedication many people wept, but Nehemiah their governor told them not to weep but rejoice in God's grace that was being shown in this new day. He said, "The joy of the Lord is your strength." Yes, we sin. Yes, there are times we suffer the consequences of sin, but there is grace in the forgiveness of Jesus Christ. There are new beginnings. We can be sorry about the past, but it does no good to continue being pulled down in guilt and bound from moving forward in the grace God provides. "The joy of the Lord is your strength."

FIRMLY IN LOVE

There are issues about people being open minded or close minded; willing to listen to other positions, or refusing to hear any other. Some Christians are accused of being closed minded fundamentalists in their condemnation of others, and there certainly are these, unfortunately. But the question is not how staunchly one holds to a position, but how he seeks to share that position. For Christians, the divinity of Christ, and salvation by faith in Him are central. These truths cannot be given up, and are worth dying for. But how we share them is of prime importance. They are first shared by a life that is lived in sacrificial service. It is only the love of Christ through us that will draw others to Him. It is being open to others, and allowing them to see that we care that will show them there is something better in Jesus. Christianity is a faith worth dying for, but more importantly it is a faith worth living to the fullest.

A QUIET SPIRIT

A saying I heard a while back said, "progress is man's attempt to complicate simplicity." Our lives do become complicated, and with the complications worries mount. "What about this? What if that happens? Will I get this done on time?" There is no easy answer to our complications, but our Lord does want to help ease our burdens. Isaiah 30:15 says, "in quietness and trust is your strength." Unfortunately, to the people to whom Isaiah wrote, he immediately followed this by saying, "but you would have none of it." Let that not be our response. Every problem we see will not be fixed today, and doesn't need to be. We make too many of our own problems by frustrating over them. Maybe quieting our tongue and quieting our mind is more what is needed. Our Lord continually invites us to quiet our soul by trusting completely in Him. Let's not borrow trouble ahead, or add more complications to life. Do what is needed for today, and leave the rest in the Lord's hands.

Pour Out Your Heart To The Lord

One of the great things about reading the Psalms is that they are completely honest. The Psalmist will praise the Lord. He will cry, complain, ask why. He trusts his God enough to let everything within him, good and bad, be completely expressed before his Lord. In one of his low times he even asked if the Lord's character had changed. "Has His lovingkindness ceased forever? Has His promise come to an end forever? Has God forgotten to be gracious, Or has He in anger withdrawn His compassion?" (Psalm 77:8-9) We simply do not and can not know all the ways of our God. Why certain things happen as they do, or why we have to suffer under very difficult trials. But then the Psalmist began to look back in his life. "Then I said, 'It is my grief, That the right hand of the Most High has changed.' I shall remember the deeds of the LORD; Surely I will remember Your wonders of old. I will meditate on all Your work And muse on Your deeds." (Psalm 77:10-12) No, God has not changed. His nature is still the deepest of love. We can't answer all of the why questions of life, but we can look back, as the Psalmist was doing here, and see all that the Lord had done for us in the past, all of the good that He has already accomplished in our life. In this we know that He has not abandoned us. Whatever we face He is the same gracious Lord, and He will see us through.

NOT THE LOTTERY TICKET

Casinos are popping up everywhere. Many store in the community have some form of numbers or "scratch off" games. The lure of hitting the next big one is always there. This is true whether with the slot machines, the lottery at the local convenience store, the mega-million jackpot, becoming the next big time talent, or even buying that latest electronic gadget. "This will solve my problems. This will make life easier. This will make me happy. With this I'll be set for life." Unfortunately, even if a big one comes in, time proves that its promises were empty. And if it doesn't come in, it only leave frustration and false hope for the "next time". There is only one real source of peace, security, and fulfillment in this world. Jesus said, "Peace I leave with you; My peace I give to you; not as the world gives do I give to you. Do not let your heart be troubled, nor let it be fearful."(John 14:27) What we seek can never be found at a gaming table, or lottery counter, but only in the One who is the source of life, and hope, Jesus, the Christ.

But In What?

Doing a little shopping in a home goods store yesterday there were a number of items on display in the checkout line. There were some small decorative pieces intended to sit on a living room table. One had the word BELIEVE written across it. Another had the word HOPE. I imagine you've seen these kinds of pieces, also. But I always have to wonder what they mean. I'm sure it is completely individual depending upon the person buying them, but the question is still valid. BELIEVE in what? HOPE in what? These are great words in the context of our faith in the Lord Jesus Christ, but outside of that they can be very vague and simply wishful thinking. They can be like the often misquoted Roman's passage (Romans 8:28) that "all things work out for good". I've heard this from a number of people in the midst of difficult situations. The verse actually says, "we know that in all things God works for the good of those who love him, who have been called according to his purpose." Belief here has a solid foundation in a relationship with our Lord through faith in Christ. On that basis our hope rests on the evidence of the love God has shown us in the redeeming work of Jesus at Calvary. Those kinds of home articles are nice decorations. Just be sure they express the depth of faith you have in the Lord.

Our Advance Person

We hear in the news about an upcoming high level meeting between heads of state. But this is not as simple a process as one leader getting on a plane and flying to the other leader's country. There are advance preparations for weeks or months before hand. The location, the number of participants, the protocol to be observed, even the type of food served and the setting of a room's furniture are planned ahead of time. Some of it may seem silly, but as little is left to chance as possible. The advance people plan out all the details. But think about our own days. We certainly do not have such high level meetings, but we do have cares and responsibilities we must encounter. I've always found it a valid pray to ask our gracious Lord to go before me this day and guide me in each situation I will face. He is our "advance person". I've also seen it a wonder and reason for thanks and praise to see the things He does in each day. Ask the Lord to go before you in this day.

Study It A Bit

When you read the Bible - please note I said when not if - don't be afraid to question the translators of a certain passage if there is something you want to understand better. Remember our Bibles are translations of the original biblical languages, and different translators will produce slightly different versions. That's why it is good to read a couple of different versions if you have a question. There are also programs that let you look at the meaning of words in the biblical Hebrew and Greek. I ran into another example of what I'm talking about here in Psalm 95:7. Both versions I generally use translate the verse, "for He is our God and we are the people of His pasture..." Yet a margin note said the literal word for "pasture" is pasturing. It may seem like splitting hairs, but it does convey a different sense of what God is doing for us. It is not just that He has a pasture He created, but it is He who is pasturing us. He is the one feeding us. God is active for our good, and not just leaving us to graze for ourselves. The Bible is God's holy word. Read it. Question what you don't understand. Look at different versions. God is feeding you.

WHAT IS GREATNESS?

Countries celebrate their important national days. They are days to honor those who serve in the military and those who have given their lives in the service of the country. These days are more than times for picnics, barbecues, and the start of a vacation. They are days of remembering the values for which those who gave their lives have fought. In the U.S. many have adopted the current slogan "Make America great again." If there was greatness to America, and I believe there was, it is only because of the values upon which our nation was founded. That foundation acknowledged God as our Creator and His Word, the Bible, as of central importance for guiding our lives. The Psalmist said it clearly, "Blessed is the nation whose God is the LORD..."^(Psalm 33:12) Is America great now? If it is, it is not because of the affluence it might provide, or its massive military might. The only greatness is in the hearts of people who are wiling to humble themselves before the Lord who made them, and to give of themselves in love for others. Greatness is only found in the two great commandments from Scripture, to love God above all else, and to love one's neighbor as one's self. (Deuteronomy 6:5f & Matthew 22:37f) "Behold, the eye of the LORD is on those who fear Him, On those who hope for His lovingkindness,..."^(Psalm 33:18)

SHOULD WE?

In the four Old Testament books called the wisdom literature, Job through Ecclesiastes, the word "wisdom" is used 103 times. We are in an age that has increased many fold in knowledge. Through the internet we have unprecedented access to information on all kinds of subjects. Unfortunately the internet does not give us wisdom. Some of those working in the highly advanced fields of study are beginning to ask the question "Just because we can do something, should we do it?" There are many questions now with the advent of Artificial Intelligence. That question can only be answered by seeking wisdom, and Scripture teaches that the source of wisdom is in the Lord. To seek that wisdom one must be willing to humble themselves before the Lord, and read and meditate upon His Word. A culture that exalts knowledge, and rejects the Lord is a culture that will destroy itself. So whether we are a researcher deeply involved in an advanced project, or just an average person trying to get through our day, we need the wisdom only our gracious Lord can give.

JUDGING A PERSON

James cautions us against making distinctions between people, valuing the rich or the beautiful over the poor and rough looking. Unfortunately this is so much a part of our fallen nature that it becomes normal to do. We were sitting in the airport terminal waiting for our short flight to Boston. In such a setting people watching is the pass time. How easy it is to judge one who is well dressed or nice looking over another. But the thought came to me. The very least of the ones I'm looking at is one whom God made in His image, and for whom our Lord gave his life. Further, we know absolutely nothing about the ones for whom we make judgments. Behind whatever appearance we see could be a great intellect, or an accomplished artist, a philanthropist, or one who gives themselves sacrificially to others. They could also be a reprobate. The point is we simply can't know, and judgment is best left up to our Lord. In that airport setting it may be a far better exercise simply to offer a brief pray for God's grace upon those we see. I'll try to keep that in mind.

The Chosen - But Why?

The Jews understood well that they were the chosen people of God. What they lost sight of was the reason for which they were chosen. In the covenant God made with Abraham, his family was to be blessed so that they in turn could be a blessing to all the nations of the earth. [Genesis 12:1-3] Jesus raised the scorn of the Jewish leaders when He went to the foreigners and outcasts. That has always been God's intent. He is not willing that any be lost, but that "all men be saved and to come to a knowledge of the truth." [I Timothy 2:4] It is still true today. The Church has been given a new covenant in Jesus Christ. We are to be a different people, but not an exclusive people. The grace that God has given us in Christ is to be extended to the world, and that world begins in our own homes, neighborhoods, and communities. It is to be extended in love in as many forms as God gives us the wisdom and inspiration. Jesus said, "if I am lifted up from the earth, I will draw all men to Myself." [John 12:32] Jesus has been lifted up in sacrifice for all people. Now we seek to lift Him up as we serve others.

First Things First

First things first. We all know that expression, but applies in many areas of life. My little grandson wants to be doing this or that right away, but he hasn't learned the basics needed to do this or that. It's all part of growing up. We are still growing up, too. We wonder/complain at time why our Lord doesn't do this, or change that, or why did He allow this to happen. But even with the Lord He has to deal with first things first. Maybe He needs to deal with some larger sin, or wrong attitude, or lack of understanding in us and others before He can change the outward thing concerning us. God deals with us as a good pastor even as Jesus did with the woman take in adultery.[(John 8)] There were probably many aspects of her life that needed to be changed, but He started by forgiving her sins and giving her a new path in life. Other things would follow. If God dealt with every wrong thing in us at once we would be crushed. He begins by declaring our forgiveness through the shed blood of His Son. In that we are set on a totally new path. Then, throughout our life He graciously touches those areas needing change. First things first.

THE LIVING GOD

When Paul preached about Jesus he always got to the part about His resurrection from the dead. This usually caused quite a stir among his listeners. In the city of Athens they took him into the great amphitheater giving him a large audience. Contrary to the various gods the Athenians worshiped Paul explained that "From one man (Adam), God made all the nations, that they should inhabit the whole earth; and he marked out their appointed times in history and the boundaries of their lands. God did this so that they would seek him and perhaps reach out for him and find him, though he is not far from any one of us."(Acts 17:26-27) In a real sense we don't find God, but God reaches out to us by the activity of His Spirit. We are surrounded by the evidence of God's creative hand. "What can be known about Him is clearly seen in all He has made."(Romans 1:20) Above all He has reveled Himself perfectly in the person of His Son, Jesus Christ. Surrounded with all the evidence of His life God calls us to open ourselves to Him more and more, and to understand that "In him we live and move and have our being."(Act 17:28) As Paul was explaining to his listeners it is this alone that begins to make sense of the daily life we live.

OUR GOD - LISTEN TO HIM

I hope that you spend time reading the Scriptures each day. Establishing a regular pattern of reading the Bible is important. Some days will seem routine and simply doing your duty, but other days will light a bright light in your mind that will make sense of what you see in life, and in all that our Lord is seeking to do with us. Psalm 81 was in my reading this morning, a prophetic passage of God speaking to Israel - and to us as the spiritual Israel. "I, the LORD, am your God, Who brought you up from the land of Egypt; Open your mouth wide and I will fill it. But My people did not listen to My voice, And Israel did not obey Me. So I gave them over to the stubbornness of their heart, To walk in their own devices. Oh that My people would listen to Me, That Israel would walk in My ways! I would quickly subdue their enemies And turn My hand against their adversaries." ^(Psalm 81:10-14) Does this make any sense? Does this say anything about our world today? Do you hear the anguish in the heart of God for His people? God really only asks one thing of us that we listen to Him. He is reaching out to us constantly and has done all that is necessary for our life and godliness. As He delivered Israel from bondage in Egypt, so He has delivered us from the bondage to sin by the atoning sacrifice of His Son, Jesus Christ. We can't change the world, but we can hear His word, and that begins the change that make a real difference.

BUT I WANT TO!

I was playing with my 4 year old grandson one Saturday. At one point I had to stop him from doing something he wanted to do. He got upset, and went off pouting as he sometimes does. I tried to explain that I wasn't scolding him, and I wasn't angry with him. I was saying this for his good. If he did what he wanted to do he could be badly hurt. He really had difficulty understanding this and still wanted to do what he had been doing - but he didn't. This is very much like the way some of God's guidance strikes us. He provides a way of life that is for our good. This doesn't always fit in with what we want to do. We may (or may not) conform to His will, but the desire is still in us to do our own thing. This is often our internal battle of wills. But if we are willing to trust our Lord who made us, and yield to His will, however hard that may be, we find that He really does have our best good at heart.

TELL YOURSELF

Do you talk to yourself? I do it frequently. There are a variety of interpretations as to why people do, but I guess for me it has just been a habit. As I read the Scripture, though, I find that I am in good company. King David in Psalm 103 said, "Praise the Lord, O my soul; and all my inmost being, praise his holy name. Praise the Lord, O my soul, and forget not all his benefits." David is reminding himself to keep his focus on the Lord. Whether we talk to ourselves or not, beginning the day with this reminder is a good way to start. We remind ourselves that our God forgives, heals, redeems, crown us with love, and satisfies us with many good things. This is the Lord we walk with daily. Whatever the task for the day, whatever the trial you face, whatever the opportunity you have, the Lord is there. Remind yourself that "the LORD is good and his love endures forever; his faithfulness continues through all generations. "(Psalm 100:5)

No "Do Overs" In Life

As kids we would play ball or other games in our backyard. Sometimes one person or another would make a bad play. We would call for a "do over" and let the person give it another try. This was great in a backyard game, but in life we don't get "do overs". Unfortunately, when something is done, it is done, and we live with the memory and whatever consequences might occur. But in life, that is in our Christian life, we have something better than a do over. We have the gracious forgiveness and cleansing of our Lord Jesus. Psalm 103:12 tells us, "as far as the east is from the west, so far has he removed our transgressions from us." Yes, memories remain, and we wish we had done things differently, but there is even another aspect of God's grace in forgiveness. He has a way of taking the bad things of the past and using them for good. God's grace is beyond measure, and is always working for our completeness in Him.

Willing To Take The Last Place

Jesus spoke with His disciples a number of time about their being wiling to take the last place, to be the servant of all. This sets up an internal battle. We don't naturally want to be last at anything - except maybe the back pews at church! We become very steeped in "our rights", what "we deserve". But we are called to set aside ourselves for the needs of others. This doesn't mean that we have a low opinion of our own worth. We are children of God for the sake of Jesus Christ. There is no higher status, and it has been given to us by pure grace. But it is a status that comes with the responsibility of service. This is not a law, but a desire and a privilege. We simply seek to extend God's grace to other. Sometimes that means getting our hand dirty doing tasks that are unpleasant, but needed. Sometimes it simply means being honest and taking responsibility for things we've done wrong, and seeking to make amends. But it does mean a willingness to die a bit more to ourselves. It is in that dying that we find life in our Lord.

A Call To The Weary And Heavy-Laden

One day Jesus' disciples were discussing who was the greatest in God's Kingdom. They, like so many of us, think about ones who accomplish great things, solve great problems, who seem to be on top of every difficulty. But Jesus responded, "Truly I say to you, unless you are converted and become like children, you will not enter the kingdom of heaven."(Matthew 18:3) We talk about child like faith, but what do we mean, what did Jesus mean? I think of my two young grandchildren. One is 4 this month, and the other almost 5. When they are tired or when they are hurt they just want to crawl up into their mother's lap and be held. There're not trying to solve great problems. They just want to be held, to have the assurance they they are loved, to know that in their mother they have a very solid figure who is the strength of their life. They just want to know that they are loved beyond measure. "But that's unrealistic for us! You don't understand the trials we face!" Is it really unrealistic? At another time Jesus said to the crowd that surrounded Him "Come to Me, all who are weary and heavy-laden, and I will give you rest. Take My yoke upon you and learn from Me, for I am gentle and. humble in heart, and you will find rest for your souls."(Matthew 11:28-29) This doesn't ignore the problems that exist, but it puts them where they belong, in the lap of our Lord where He can give comfort, strength, clarity for all of our needs. We need to know that we are surrounded by His love.

OUR REASON FOR BEING

What is necessary for life? Certainly air, water, and food are essential to sustain physical life. Along with rest and exercise, these keep the body moving, but life is more than the physical body. We need a reason for being. Animals survive by nature and instinct, but humans ponder the question of purpose. Why am I here? To answer this, we need fellowship with other humans to give us a sense of belonging, and we need faith to show us that there is something beyond our brief span of years. We are not self made, and we are not self sufficient. Our God, the Father of our Lord Jesus Christ, invites us to find our meaning in Him. There are many world faiths. This shows the hunger in man for meaning. But true meaning is only found in the One who loved us enough to reveal Himself personally in Jesus Christ. That is what Christmas is about. By growing deeper in our life with Jesus we find meaning for life. And that is more necessary than just sustaining physical life.

THE WONDER OF IT ALL

We speak of the wonder of the Christmas Season particularly in the eyes of children. All of the decorations, colored lights, and friendly gatherings make this a very special time. Unfortunately, as we grow older we face all of the hassles and losses of life. The wonder is tainted by life's realities. But that is the very point of the marvelous wonder of this Christmas time. Almighty God came into this world with all its work, hassles, and losses not only to experience all that we experience, but to redeem our lives in the midst of them. Christmas is far more than decorated trees and sales at the mall. Christmas, above all is Emmanuel, God with us. This is the wonder of all wonders. The joy of all joys. That Almighty God has loved you personally so much that He sent His only Son into your life to pay the penalty for all your sins, and to give you the assurance that, whatever your good times or bad, He will never leave or forsake you. Christmas is Emmanuel, God with us. Don't ever lose the wonder of that truth.

WE GET WHAT WE WANT

We get what we want, but it isn't always good for us. The temptation to misuse the gift of our sexuality has been with us since the first fall of mankind from the will of God. But now, through our technologies and "advanced understanding" (I obviously write that with a sarcastic tone) we have removed sexuality from the intended act of marital joy and procreation within a covenant marriage. We've declared this to be a great advance for human life. While people have a lot of fun with their freedom, statistics show that this has not led to greater happiness and satisfaction in life. And it has led to a lot of harm. Marriage, which has been shown to bring more happiness and security, has been delayed or not entered into at all. National birthrates aren't even at replacement levels, and the increasing elder population has put a great strain on society. The point of all this again shows the truth that God, our Designer, knew what he was doing when He first created us. We were made for marriage, sex within its confines, family, commitment, and care beyond our own personal satisfaction. It is all in God's holy word. We really should take it a bit more seriously. No, getting what we want really is not always for our good.

By Deeds Of Love

The Scripture teaches that a laborer is worthy of his hire. Paul wrote that "the Lord has commanded that those who preach the gospel should receive their living from the gospel. (1Corinthians 9:14) Paul also wrote to Timothy, one of his most faithful ministers, that "if we have food and clothing, we will be content with that."(1Timothy6:8) That doesn't mean that ministers of the Gospel have to live the most austere life. Also, it does take money for the various aspects of sharing the word of Christ to the world. But there is something wrong with a television evangelist asking followers to donate $54 million for a new private jet. $54 million could do a lot more in many other areas of care for the Lord's people. It also gives the church as whole a bad name, and denies the truth of the grace of God as a free gift of new life in Jesus Christ. We have the greatest possible message to share with the world. It is a truth best shared in actions of love, and words of grace from one believer to another. That has nothing to do with $54 million jets.

GLUED TO THE SCREEN

As people observe the conditions in our world today one will hear references to George Orwell's book 1984. While he is off by 30 plus year many of the things he wrote in his fictional account of life under a Big Brother government seem rather prophetic. He foresaw total control by the rewriting of history and propagating false news. The general society was placated by having their fill of shallow entertainment, and alcohol. There was an article in our local paper yesterday entitled "The internet's cute tranquilizer". The article highlighted a Pew Research study that said "25 percent of all U.S. adults are constantly on line and 77 percent of all Americans to online multiple time a day. With this kind of immersive mind-meld in full effect, our attention spans dry up...as technology provides even-more stimulation, we find ourselves panicked by (any loss of service)...there are far more serious things for us to worry about..." but as long as we are happy with our gadgets much can be ignored. I am certainly not opposed to all uses of the internet. After all I'm using it right now, but for many the writer has a real point. Can we use the technologies we are given, and not lose the ability to observe, to think critically, and to interact meaningfully, and personally with other individuals?

ANCHOR POINTS

I think at various time we all struggle with the difference between the things we see with our eyes, and the things we believe but can't see. That's where our faith is. We believe in our Lord. We believe He loves us. We believe He cares about all our needs. But we can't see Him, and we are staring at this need, this problem that is right in front of us. The Lord has told us not to worry, not to be anxious, to trust Him...and we do, but we still struggle. This is where a couple of things are important to remember. One, we are not alone, we are part of a fellowship of believes who walk with us through life. They counsel us, encourage us, pray for us, provide material support when needed. And two, we look back in our lives seeing where the Lord has worked in our past. I call these the anchor points of faith. We know God did certain thing, provided certain things, gave a peace in a difficult situation - the examples of numerous - but we Know that God acted then in that time even if it was years past. We believe He will not abandon us in this need. We walk day by day with our Lord, beyond physical sight, but very real, and completely sufficient for all our days.

An After Death Experience

We have probably all read or heard some of those after death experiences people report. People are clinically dead for a period of time, brought back to life, and report what they saw. I don't put too much stock in many of these, but there is one after death experience that is important for all of us who confess faith in Jesus Christ. Paul wrote to the Ephesian church, "You were dead in your transgressions and sin in which you used to live...(Ephesians 2:1) But then he goes on to explain, "because of His great love for us, God who is rich in mercy, made us alive with Christ even when we were dead in transgressions..."(Ephesians 4&5) By faith in Jesus Christ we have all died to sin and been raised to a new life in Christ. It is in that life we live each day. A common characteristic of the reported after death experiences is that people are no longer afraid of death. Our certainty in Christ is more sure. We have died and been raised again. We are already living in resurrected life. We need not fear the transition at physical for "nothing can separate us from the love of God in Christ Jesus our Lord".(Romans 8:39)

Our Home Field Advantage

Living near Baltimore and Washington as we do we are surrounded by a number of sports teams. Often one or the other of the teams will make it to a playoff series, as the Washington Capitals are in now. During the series games are played here and in the opponents city. People talk about the "home field advantage". That mean the stadium is filled with local fans cheering for the team. A special measure of encouragement often makes the difference. That is what we, as Christians, are about. It is why the Church is called a body, all parts are members one of another, and need one another. We are brothers and sisters together in the faith. "If one part suffers, every part suffers with it; if one part is honored, every part rejoices with it." (1 Corinthians 12:26) Times can be difficult. We pray for one another. We encourage one another. We lift burdens together. Sometimes we just quietly stand along side another. In Christ Jesus we are always reminded that we have the home field advantage.

WONDERFULLY MADE

I have done a lot of woodworking over the years so I know a lot of the processes for constructing furniture. I enjoy looking at some antique pieces, but when I see an intricate secretary or a breakfront from two or three hundred years ago I have no idea how it was made. I marvel at the craftsmanship. Audrey and I were in an orthopedic doctor's office yesterday. There were six of those wall charts of various parts of the human body lining the wall. One was even labeled "The Amazing Back". I marveled at the incredible complexity of the human body. So complex we have to have specialists for each part, and even they don't know it all. Then I thought "my God made that!". He knows every joint, mussel, and organ in our whole body. That is the magnitude of my God and your God. And even more, he cares about the soul and spirit of each body He has made. He cares enough to redeem it by the precious blood of His only begotten Son. Having done all that He can be trusted for what is ahead of us in this day. Our God. Amazing love.

Not Sufficient Alone

As I get older I become more aware of my limits. I need help with various things. I am not sufficient in myself. I depend on the strength and wisdom of God, and that which He sends me through others. I can't identify with the self-made or self sufficient person. I am too aware of my limits. Yet, while I am weak, I praise our gracious Lord because His strength is sufficient for all needs. This is true not just with aging. As I look back over my life I realize all of the times God sent people to help me that made a vast difference in my direction. Nothing that I planned, but help needed at the time. It is necessary from me to realize this. It keeps me from being puffed up with pride, or rating my accomplishments higher than they should be. Thinking like this we come back to the Potter and Clay image of Jeremiah 18. God is the One shaping us into vessels for His use. We can put lumps in our pile of clay that impede His progress, but in His great love He continues to work. At every age He is our help, making us into vessels for His glory.

ARE YOU NEEDY?

We do what we can to help the needy. We are aware of needs for food and shelter in our own country. We give what we can. Our church is currently working on a project to help a church in Tanzania. So, we are aware of various needs, and try to help. But there is a deeper question. Are you needy? We probably don't think of ourselves that way. Most of us have a lot more things than we really need, and as far as food is concerned that is pretty abundant. There is another sense in which it is necessary that we see ourselves as needy. David, King of Israel, had an abundance of material things, but he would write, "Hear me, LORD, and answer me, for I am poor and needy. Guard my life, for I am faithful to you; save your servant who trusts in you. You are my God; have mercy on me, Lord, for I call to you all day long. Bring joy to your servant, Lord, for I put my trust in you." (Psalm 86:1-4) We are not sufficient in ourselves to live a life pleasing to our Lord. We are daily dependent upon the grace of God for understanding, wisdom, guidance, and strength. It is only in seeing ourselves as needy that we continue to "walk humbly with our God". (Micah 6:8)

WHO ARE YOU?

Who are you? Obviously you have a name indicating your family background. There are numerous other items that describes who you are. But one above all is vital. The Apostle Paul writes to the Ephesian Church that you "were once darkness and now you are light in the Lord". (Ephesians 5:8) I always thought this a striking statement. It is not "you were in darkness", but "you were darkness". That was your identity. That is who you were. In our sin we were nothing but darkness, and there was nothing we could do to change it. If we were just "in darkness" we could walk out, but Paul is saying that is not the case. Darkness is who you were. It is only the redeeming blood of Jesus Christ that brought light into your life. "This is not from yourselves, it is the gift of God." (Ephesians 2:8) We can't claim anything from the Lord. We can only rejoice in the wonder of what He has done. Now you are light in the Lord. Live as children of the light. That is who you are.

To Live Is Christ

St. Paul wrote in Philippians 1:21 "For me to live is Christ and to die is gain." I attended a funeral of a pastor in our community. Bud had been in this area for almost 50 years. There was no one else I know that could be called the town's pastor. He had a local church, but he knew, and had ministered to, most of the business owners and many others in the town. He didn't have an easy life. He and his family always lived on a very tight budget, faced a number of family problems, and had been driven from one church by internal conflict. Yet for him to live was Christ. It was a joy to meet and talk with him. The name of Jesus was in his heart and on his lips. The packed church testified to the impact the Lord had on many through his life. And the funeral service was glorious! For him to die was truly gain. Paul's words are not just for preachers. He was writing to a normal Christian congregation. What he said is a witness for us all. Life is not easy. Trials abound. Yet Jesus Christ is in the midst of life, and by His Spirit He is in the midst of us. To live is Christ, and death is not feared. It can only be gain.

NOT THE LAST WORD

When one reads the newspaper or internet headlines they always seem to lead with the bad news. The latest murder, traffic accident, scandal, flood or tornado. I know those things are there. We do need to know what is going on and take proper precautions where necessary. We live in a broken world, and that brokenness touches all of us in a variety of ways. But that is never the end of the story, and it should not be the lead story in our minds. In whatever situation we find ourselves we are in our Father's hands. Jesus has told us not to worry, not to be anxious, to put complete trust in our gracious Lord. No, it is not easy in the face of fearful things. There is strength in Jesus. We are called to patience, and hope in our Lord who has shown His love for us in many ways. Rather than the latest headlines how about reading[Philippians 4:4-8].

PEACE?

At one of the most uncertain times in the lives of Jesus' disciples He said, "Peace I leave with you; my peace I give you. I do not give to you as the world gives. Do not let your hearts be troubled and do not be afraid. [John 14:27] That is a wonderful thought, but it also leaves us with a question. How do we get there? How do we have that kind of peace? I think it is something we all want. There is a supernatural peace that the Lord gives at certain very difficult times in life. It is an assurance of His presence and care. But we who believe in the Lord Jesus Christ are also to be purveyors of peace. How can we, in the normal course of our day, bring a sense to peace to the places where we are? It starts with our own eyes focused in trust on Jesus. The more we look to Him in in trust and hope the more His peace will reflect through us wherever we are.

BUMPER STICKERS

We've all seen a variety of sayings on bumper stickers. Some are humorous, others caustic. Some are intended to make us think, or inspire to action. A fairly common one is "Practice random acts of kindness". A good admonition. Another I saw on the tire cover on the back of a Jeep - "Life is Good". It made me think about the depth of some of these slogans. By themselves they contain some truth, but ultimately are pretty shallow. Acts of kindness are certainly commendable wherever they are found. But they are not going to start of crusade of kind actions that changes the world. It doesn't recognize the sin that resides in each heart that can only be changed by Jesus. Life is good, certainly, but can we say that in the midst of a tragedy? Only if we understand that our Lord is in the midst of all life giving strength in good times and in bad. Slogans can be fun, but let them stir you to think more deeply than the surface sentiment. What do they mean in our life with Christ?

THREE IN ONE

Talking with one of my people a while back they were saying it was difficult for them to pray to God, the Father. They had no image of the unseen Father they could visualize. This friend said all their prayers were to Jesus who was a clear picture of a person for them. I think all of us struggle a bit with explaining or visualizing God as three persons of the Holy Trinity, yet only one God. I've likened it at times to an ant trying to understand a human. But God, who desires a true relationship with us, in the depth of His grace, did what only He could do to make Himself known. Paul wrote "...Christ Jesus, being in very nature God,... made himself nothing by taking the very nature of a servant, being made in human likeness."(Phillippians 2:5-7) Jesus is God. In theology we say the second person of the Holy Trinity, but Jesus is the way we know who God is and what He is like. All of the Bible is centered in the person of Jesus Christ. The concept is God, the Holy Trinity, is important, but my friend was doing well to direct their devotion to Jesus.

In Debt? Yes!

I've listened to a few financial programs on the radio where people call in for advice. It is not uncommon for a caller to have a credit card debt of tens of thousands of dollars and want to know what to do. We also hear it today with student loan debt. Suppose the one to whom the debt was owed would come and simply cancel it. How would one feel about such a gift? A debt far too high to pay has just been canceled. That is just what our Lord has done for us. Paul wrote to the Colossian Christians that God has "canceled out the (our) certificate of debt ". (Colossians 2:14) In the original language the "certificate of debt" is a legal term, an official document, just as binding as any business loan. But this debt, our debt to the Lord, is so great it is totally impossible for us to pay. The thirteenth verse says that "we were dead in our sins". Our debt of sin had totally separated us from God and there was nothing, nothing we could do about it. But God, in His amazing grace, took our certificate of debt and in the blood of Jesus Christ wrote "canceled" across it. People with a canceled credit card debt might say they have been given a new lease on life. For us, we have literally been given a new life, made alive in Jesus.

WORK HEARTILY

What do you have on your schedule for today? We generally have a series of items on our list, some required, some flexible, some for fun. Paul wrote "Whatever you do, work at it with all your heart, as working for the Lord, not for men..." (Colossians 3:23) Think about that along with your To Do list. We do the best we can in whatever the task to give honor to Jesus. Is this a normal work day? You are working for Jesus and not for the company. Are you a caregiver at home? You are serving in the love of Jesus and to Him. Are you grocery shopping? Not always fun, but in Jesus' name it is to Him and for the good of the household. Are you just kicking back and relaxing? That too is for the Lord in renewing the body He created. Is the task pleasant, or frustrating, or just routine daily living? It is all in the Lord. He gives us our day and the grace we need for it. We do it heartily as to the Lord.

SO BIG!

Many years ago J.B. Phillips wrote a small book called Your God Is Too Small. In it he outlined various people's views of how they see God - as a policeman enforcing laws, as a benevolent grandfather, and so forth. All of these are inadequate and as Phillips said, "too small". He may have aspects of each of these small views, but we dare not confine Him to any one of them. God is a God of perfect justice displayed in the commandments He has given for life. God is a God of perfect love displayed in the redemptive cross He has given that we might be a part of Him. He is not a God that can be made light of. He will not overlook sin and rebellion forever. But He is a God who invites us to come and find our true life and peace in Him. Above all He is our God who calls us to trust Him for all times of life even when we can't understand the full magnitude of His being or see the extent of His will for us. He is a God who can be trusted.

Agents Of The Kingdom

Jesus preached "repent for the Kingdom of God is at hand". Many of his parables began "the Kingdom of God is like...". What is this Kingdom He is talking about? We believe there is an eternal Kingdom. We speak of going to heaven when we die. But there is another aspect of the Kingdom that is important now. Because of the atoning sacrifice of Jesus paying the penalty for our sins we have been brought into God's Kingdom now. It is a growing reality in our hearts. Paul wrote, "For He rescued us from the domain of darkness, and transferred us to the kingdom of His beloved Son,..."(Colossians 1:13) The Kingdom is not out there in the sweet by and by. We are agents of God's Kingdom today sharing the truth and grace of that Kingdom in daily words and actions. Just as Jesus and the disciples shared the Good News throughout Israel, so you and I, with the presence of Jesus, share the Good News in our part of the world.

THEOLOGY MATTERS, BUT.....

I'm reading an account of a Christian who is serving in a very difficult and dangerous position. He is very faithful in practicing his faith, and receives much abuse for it. He is part of a Christian denomination with which I have many theological disagreements. However, it is clear that he is not just slavishly following teachings of his denomination. All this man does is in trust of God, obedience to the Scriptures, and to honor his Lord. And it is obvious that the Lord has blessed him and answered a number of very important prayers at critical times in his life. It is not that theology doesn't matter. It does, but the centrality of the atoning work of Jesus Christ is heart to all true Christian faiths. Paul wrote to the Romans that "one person regards one day above another, another regards every day alike. Each person must be fully convinced in his own mind".[14:5] Each one, Paul says, is doing it to honor the Lord. Our differences do matter, and provide opportunities were we can study, discuss and grow, and sometimes just live with the differences. They should not be reasons to condemn others who are acting in an honest faith to bring glory to our Lord.

Proper Discernment

I want to pick up on the last sentence of the Good Morning I wrote yesterday. I was writing about the differences that exist between Christian denominations. I wrote, "They should not be reasons to condemn others who are acting in an honest faith to bring glory to our Lord." First, we never have the right to "condemn" individuals. That means to judge with damnation. That is only God prerogative, not ours. However, we are not freed from making right judgments according to God's Word. Some behaviors, some teaching, are directly contrary to the truth God has given us in His Word. For the strength of the Body of Christ such things must be confronted and declared wrong. There are some things that bring honor to God and some things that clearly do not. At times it's a difficult call, and it is not done with the intention of driving anyone away, but that that person might be restored to full fellowship. Paul tells us to "teach and admonish one another with all wisdom... (Colossians 3:16) Our desire, whether individually or in our chosen Christian denomination, is to bring glory to our Lord Jesus Christ, and to show others the path to life.

An Important Pinch And Dash

I am not much of a cook, but I can make a good omelet, some pancakes, and follow a recipe when I need to. I see herbs and spices on the rack at the grocery store. I know nothing about these. I understand that a pinch of this or a dash of that can make a big difference in a well prepared meal, but that is way beyond me. When it comes to the Bible, however, I do know and greatly appreciate that a pinch of this or a dash of that can make a huge difference. What I mean is that we don't ignore those little things. The way a phrase is stated, a word or two in the midst of a sentence. This is God's Holy Word, our food for life. God is the Master Chef and His Word has a rich flavor. It can't be gobbled down as too many of us are accustomed to do. It is to be savored, studied, meditated upon. The nourishment that comes in its pages are like no other.

Given And Shed For You

I've been attending the national convention of our church denomination all this week. One of the hallmarks of our time together is worship, morning and evening. Tonight we shared a service of Holy Communion. Probably not all that different from services you attend. There is music, the reading of Scripture, and the consecration of the Sacrament. The Celebrant declares in the words of Scripture, "Jesus took bread, broke it, and gave it to the disciples saying 'this is my body given for you.' Then He took the cup instructing all to drink of it, saying 'this is the new covenant in my blood shed for you.'" The bread and wine are then distributed to the congregation. I was sitting near the front, within ten feet of the Celebrant who was distributing the bread as people filed by. I heard him repeat, probably a hundred time, "This is the true Body of Christ given unto death for your sins". The words couldn't have been more clear. In this bread, in this cup, I received the forgiveness of all my sins. Whatever had gone before in my life; whatever thoughts or actions I had done or failed to do, were gone. They were cleansed in the broken body and shed blood of my Savior. I was free. And not only me, that broken body and shed blood redeemed you, and all mankind. In Christ you are free. Those are the most serious and most freeing words spoken on earth - given and shed for you for the forgiveness of your sins. Hear them and live in the Joy of your Lord.

In A Few Words

Sometimes one does not need a lot of words. In fact, brevity and clarity are often best. (Who said I should take my own advice!) But I was thinking of the shortest of the hundred and fifty Psalms, number 117.

"Praise the LORD, all you nations; extol him, all you peoples. For great is his love toward us, and the faithfulness of the LORD endures forever. Praise the LORD." It is not that God needs our praise. He is complete in Himself, but we need to praise and extol Him. In so doing we draw near to His life, and strengthen our faith. These few words emphasize His great love, a personal love and faithfulness that is beyond our full comprehension. Yet a love that endures. It is a love that points forward to the greatest expression of that love in the atoning sacrifice of Christ on our behalf. It's all there, and much to meditate upon in just two short verses.

No Substitute

We use substitutes for many things. Making a recipe and don't have one ingredient, we find what can be substituted. Buying a prescription we ask to substitute the generic because it is cheaper. A teacher is absent we call in a substitute. Even famous people have doubles who substitute for them in certain situations. This is all quite common and reasonable, but we need to be careful when we extend it to our Lord. Jesus said, "I have come that you may have life and have it more abundantly." (John 10:10) That life is found in love and trust of our Lord, but too often we make substitutes. We love other things more than Jesus. We trust Him, but we hedge our bets, having alternatives if He doesn't come through. The commandment says we are to have no other gods before Him, but we often do. Our God loves us with an everlasting love, and really is working daily for our best good. There can be no substitute for that.

ARE YOU FREE?

In our Declaration of Independence from our Founding Fathers stated that we have "inalienable rights" to life, liberty, and the pursuit of happiness. For political purposes this sounds wonderful, and it has worked in our democratic system for a lot of years. But that is really not a definition of true freedom. There are millions of free people in our country that are in bondage, to addictions, to finances, to any number of other things mentally and physically. True free is something quite apart from the ability to do whatever we want. Jesus said,"If you hold to my teaching,... Then you will know the truth, and the truth will set you free."(John 8:31-32) True freedom is living in conformity to God's will. It is in knowing and yielding to the love of God in Christ Jesus, our Lord. One who is living in Christ is free regardless of his or her outward circumstances. Political freedom is nice, and we seek to preserve it, but freedom in Christ is paramount. For without that we really are in bondage no matter what our outward condition.

WHY?

Many people like mysteries, dramas on TV, books by mystery writers, and so forth. But these mysteries always have a solution, usually with the good guys coming out on top. But where we don't like mysteries is in our Christian faith. It is the reason the "why" question comes up so often. Why did God do this or allow that? Or in our sacraments. Jesus said "this is my body, this is my blood", but we want to explain if or how it really is. It is hard for us to take God at his word, and trust that what He says is true without an explanation. It all began back in the Garden. God said "don't eat of the tree" and we wanted to know why. But the heart of faith is taking God at His word, trusting Him, and believing He is our good Father.

What Is Needed?

At times the prophets pointed to the foolishness of the things we do. Isaiah uses the illustration of a man who plants trees on his land. He cares for them until they grow strong. Then when one is ready he cuts it down. "It is used as fuel for burning; some of it he takes and warms himself, he kindles a fire and bakes bread. But he also fashions a god and worships it; he makes an idol and bows down to it."(Isaiah 44:15) The same wood he grew has many useful purposes, but then he also makes an idol out of the same wood and worships it as his god. We laugh. How foolish. But then we think a little more deeply and it begins to bite with its truth. We are not far from there with our own creations. It becomes fairly easy to get caught up in science, technology, lifestyles we've created for ourselves, and any number of other things. Do they serve a needful purpose for us, for which we give things to Almighty God for His gifts? Or do we serve them as a necessary part of life? Mary knelt at Jesus' feet, while Martha fretted over all the work she had to do. Jesus said, "Mary has chosen the best portion..."(Luke 10:42) Let's be sure we, too, choose the best portions.

By The Thousands

Angles are interesting. When one flies over the mid-west looking out at the farm fields everything is in perfect squares or rectangles. This is very efficient, and easy to drive around. It is not so in the east. There are all kinds of curves, and angles to the roads and fields. I must admit I find the squares and rectangles rather boring. Just the same as I miss the hills and valleys when I get out to the flatter lands. As far as the land is concerned, it's all good. God gave us all of this for our benefit. It just reminds me that God in into variety, beauty, and many interesting things. If God had wanted to give us some pretty flowers He could have created a few, or a dozen or two. But He made many thousands, all different, many beautiful, some even whimsical. I learned yesterday that there are over 3000 kinds of mosquitoes! Angles are interesting, so are curves, squares, not to mention color variations in each thing we see. It is God's gift of beauty and life. Look around and let it all return to our Father in praise.

MANY SERMONS ARE AROUND US

When driving, especially on a longer trip, I love to look around at the interesting things along the roadway. One time I was driving back from a youth conference in Minneapolis with two of my kids. This was a pre-Iphone time, and I had something of a captive audience as we drove through Wisconsin, and Illinois farm country. It was mid-day on a Sunday and I gave them a half hour sermon on the style of barn roofs. I'll tell you about that sometime, but my point is that there is much to see in the world God has given us. Life, and the people God brings across our paths, even casually, can teach us much. We are all sinful beings redeemed only by the grace of God. We live in a world broken by rebellion from God's will. Yet, there is much beauty and good that our Lord desires us to see. And further, we have beauty and good we can contribute. Jesus said, "You are the light of the world. let your light shine before others, that they may see your good deeds and glorify your Father in heaven."(Matthew 5:14-16) There really is much to see - and to give - in God's world.

Solid And Lasting

When I have a wedding, as part of the wedding message I emphasize the characteristics of love, especially that true love is based on actions and not on feelings. This is an important understanding for all life. We have many things to do each day. Not all of them are fun, or make us feel good, but we do them because they are necessary and it is the right thing to do. Our lives are to be governed by principles, and by seeking to do good for others. As Christians, our principles come from our understanding of our Lord and His Holy Word. So we do what we believe is right whether it is pleasant or not. But the amazing thing with seeking to live by our Lord's principles is that we do find great joy and blessing. God does want us to feel good. All the bells and whistles that come with a wedding and beginning married life are great, but that is not our goal. We are in this life for the long haul, and having God's joy is far more precious.

SECURITY

Security may be one of the biggest words in our society right now. The government is working hard to provide security against terror attacks. Companies are concerned about security on their computer systems. We have passwords to get into our own computer files. And certainly there is the concern for health and financial security. We work very hard at it all. But there is really only one ultimate security, and that is through faith in Jesus Christ. Faith in the One who said, "don't be anxious", (Matthew 6:25) who promised us that "He would never leave or forsake us". (Hebrews 13:5) It is in this security, security in Him, that we can go about our days without fear. Thank be to God through Jesus Christ our Lord.

Tools In God's Hand

Each week at our time of prayer in out worship service we pray for the president and the leaders of our nation. We are taught in Scripture to pray for our leaders so that we may lead an orderly and productive life. We have no allusion that all of our leaders are Christians or are guided by Biblical principles, but, by the presence of God's Spirit, He can still use them for His good purpose. After all Cyrus the Great, king of Persia five centuries before Christ was a pagan ruler, yet God called him "my shepherd and (he) will accomplish all that I please;..." God used Cyrus for the good of His people. [(Isaiah 44 and 45)] We pray that God will work in our leaders even beyond what they themselves understand. It is also our prayer that God's Spirit will open hearts and minds to be receptive to His word, and find the truth of His saving grace. We have the promise that when God's Word goes forth it "will accomplish what I desire and achieve the purpose for which I sent it." [(Isaiah 55:11)] "For the word of God is living and active and sharper than any two-edged sword,..." [(Hebrews 4:12)] So we pray for our leaders, and we pray that God's Spirit will enlighten many hearts and minds.

Build On A Solid Foundation

When our grandson got engaged. It was complete with a romantic setting, down on one knee, and a beautiful ring. Old fashioned by today's standards, but important none the less. They are not living together. There is no "trial marriage". They have taken a couple of years to get to know one another. They have talked much, and had counseling from the church even before the engagement. When it was finally time to propose, and his girl accepted, it was a commitment. They were saying "I want to spend the rest of my life with you, to support you and care for you always". This is the solid foundation for beginning a marriage. It is not the bells, whistles, and warm fuzzies that hold a couple together, but the commitment to give of one's self completely in all the coming circumstances. No, it doesn't always work, but in God's grace it is the right way. In our modern culture girls give themselves away far too easily, reaping many tears, and guys are eager to take advantage of it. Maybe we should set aside our focus on self gratification, and look back to some of the solid traditions of the past, seeking to live lives the way our Lord intended.

GOD'S CHILD

Paul wrote to the Roman church, "Do not think of yourself more highly than you ought, but rather think of yourself with sober judgment, in accordance with the faith God has distributed to each of you."(Romans 12:3) As in all things there is a balance. Jesus looked for humility and trust. No one likes an egotistical person who inflates himself above everyone else. But at the same time we should not depreciate ourselves. We are children of God, created in His image, and beloved. This is not of ourselves. It is God's gift and calling. We can look at ourselves as God's child for Jesus sake. We can recognize that He has given us certain gift, thing that we do well - probably not better than others, but we do have talents and abilities that are good. We use them to the best of our ability, and to God's glory. We can take pride in a job well done, but that pride is above all in our God who is "the giver of every good and perfect gift..."(James 1:17)

THE PURPOSE OF KNOWLEDGE - TRUE PROGRESS

There are times when reading Scripture that a verse will stand out with a special truth. It's those time we might say, "right on!". Such a verse stood out for me recently. Paul had been listing a long series of bad characteristics of people in the last days of the Church age. He concludes the list by saying they are "always learning but never able to come to a knowledge of the truth."(II Timothy 3:7) It seems quite descriptive to me. We are certainly in an age where learning is increasing at an exponential rate. There are things being done today that have never been done before. It is as God said of the people seeking to build the Tower of Babel, if they continue as one language "nothing will be impossible for them".(Genesis 11:6) We have substantially overcome the language barrier, and are back on the path of Babel. But knowledge has become totally man centered and not God centered. God is the source of all knowledge, and unless our knowledge is God directed, and draws us closer to Him, it only leads to confusion. This is the myth of progress. The only true progress is that which leads us to a deeper understanding of our Creator.

The Purpose of Knowledge - Strengthen Our Relationship

I opened up a subject yesterday that leads to a lot of different discussions. I had said, "unless our knowledge is God directed, and draws us closer to Him, it only leads to confusion", also remarking that our search for knowledge has become completely man centered and not God centered. There are numerous commission and committees established to answer the moral question, "Just because we can do it, should we do it?". This was very prominent at the time cloning was so much in the news. But it can apply to a number of areas, not just bio-ethics. I've always said everything goes back to Genesis. It is the same question posed to Adam's mind at the Tree of the Knowledge of Good and Evil, "Just because I am able to eat of this fruit, should I?". Each time he denied himself he gave honor to God, and strengthened his relationship with Him. Of course we know that he yielded to temptation as so many are today in biological and other areas. The question always remain - just because I can, should I? Never an easy question to answer. But the more we keep our desire on strengthening our relations with Christ, the more we will answer it correctly.

FULLY WASHED

Most TV commercials are pretty silly, but some have a completely unintended point. There is currently one about a laundry soap that has a good line. A young man is on a date. His girlfriend calls attention to his shirt which is wrinkled and out of shape. The commercial say, "that's when you know it is only half washed". Well, I don't know what something being half washed in the laundry means, but think about the other washing that is essential to our lives - being washed in the blood of Jesus. It is only His sacrifice on the cross that has made us clean and able to stand in His pure white robe of righteousness before God. Our modern world works hard to get rid of the name of Jesus and the symbol of the cross. We try all other means to make ourselves acceptable to God, but that's like being half washed. And as the young fellow really wasn't acceptable to his girlfriend, it is not the way we are acceptable to our God. Jesus, the second person of the Holy Trinity, the Son of Almighty God became one of us. "He humbled himself by becoming obedient to death- even death on a cross!" (Philippians 2:8) God did this that we might be redeemed from the power of sin, death, and the devil. This is the true and full washing that gives us eternal life. Anything else is trying to get by being half washed.

Our Life Is Worship

What is worship? Well, of course, it is something you do when you go to church on Sundays. You sing, listen to scripture, hear a sermon, and receive communion. That is all part of worship. But worship is far more, and is by no means limited to Sundays. Worship is an attitude of the heart in humble submission to our gracious Lord. It is acknowledging and clinging in grateful love to the One who has made us and given us life. Worship is different from praise. Praise is the outward response in the words and actions of our daily life to the One we worship. Sunday is only one expression of worship. We live in worship every hour of every day as we bow in our hearts to the God of all creation. Look forward to your time of worship, fellowship and praise on Sunday, but live in the worship of our Lord always.

Longing To Return

We have a small train platform under our Christmas tree. It has just one oval track with the Lionel train I had as a kid. My grandkids love to play with it. I also have a number of miniature trees, people, animals, and things that came from my father when he was young. I enjoy creating a small park setting, children playing, older folks relaxing on a park bench, and so forth. For some reason its always been a snow scene, pure white. It strikes me, as I looked at it again this morning, that I, or we, try to create an idealistic image of life. It is the same as looking at a Thomas Kinkade painting or a Currier and Ives greeting card. It points to a desire, an internal longing, for an age of peace, happiness, beauty, and perfection. We may not realize it or think of it in that way, but ever since we were driven from the Garden because of our sin we have had a longing to return to that place of perfection and relationship with our Lord. We talk about Christmas as a time of peace and good will, but it is far more. It is God coming among us to provide the way, the only means, by which we can return to the life for which we long. Jesus said, "I have come that you may have life and have it to the full.^(John 10:10) We do not yet see our life complete, but in Jesus Christ we will.

"

With Prayer And Deeds

On one of his missionary journeys Paul went to Thessalonica, Berea, and to Athens to preach the Gospel. In Thessalonica the people were contentious and argumentative. In Berea they were willing to search the Scriptures to see if what Paul was saying was correct. In Athens they wanted to philosophize and kick around some new idea. Things really haven't changed when we try to share the Gospel. Among all of our friends and acquaintances, each hears and receives things a bit differently. Some are Thessalonicans, some Bereans, and so forth. We have the commission, and the desire to share God's truth with others. But this is why it is often better to not start with words, but with prayer and with actions. As we live our faith, and as we pray for others, God will prepare hearts, and bring to us those who ask about what they see in us. Then we can share what the Lord means in our lives. God can sort out the different folks for us.

We Don't Need Horoscopes

Friday the 13th is supposed to be an unlucky day. I don't know the origin of that superstition, and I'm not that interested to look it up. My mother was born on a Friday the 13th so I know it isn't all bad. There are many such superstitions from black cats, to going under ladders, to knocking on wood. The list can be endless. People read their horoscope to see if their day will be good or not. But all of this is something that should be far from us. Such false practices and false gods were the downfall of ancient Israel and strictly forbidden by the Lord. And while it is not so bad to jokingly knock on wood when we hope something good will happen it should remind us that we have all the truth and guidance we need in God's holy word, and the presence of His Holy Spirit. The Lord Jesus Christ is our life, our strength and our hope. So have a blessed day today in the Lord no matter what number is on it.

Feeling Close To God

I have heard people say that they feel close to God when in church on Sunday morning. In the singing and the prayers, God seemed to be very near. This is fine, and we are admonished in Scripture to "not neglect the meeting together." (Hebrews10:25) Although, coming to church is far more than how we feel about it. My girls go to get their nails and toes done when they want to feel good. It is important that we receive a blessing from our time of corporate worship, but that blessing is far more than how we feel. There is an objective reality in our time of worship as we hear the proclamation of the Gospel, the truth of God's love for us in Jesus Christ. We receive the visible demonstration of His forgiving grace as we receive His body and blood in the Holy Communion. These are the real blessings in our time of worship, independent of how we feel that day. God has come to you in Jesus Christ. I hope you do feel good as you worship together with fellow believers. But it is just that our feelings are not the reason for worship. God's true and continuing grace upon us is.

SEEING IS BELIEVING - REALLY?

Some people have trouble believing in something that they can't see, or can't apprehend with their physical senses. Yet we do it all the time. For example, many people have TV service by satellite today. 250 plus channels! Why anyone needs that many is beyond me, but that's not my point here. We look at the dish receiving antennas attached to many houses, and coming into those antennas are more that 250 simultaneous images. No one can see them, but they are there and we take them for granted. Physics can explain electro-magnetic wave propagation, but it is still beyond our five senses, yet we believe in it. We say we see the results of it on the TV screen, therefore it must be real. We see the results of it! But we also see the activity of our Lord all around us. Paul speaks to this saying, "For since the creation of the world, God's invisible qualities—his eternal power and divine nature—have been clearly seen, being understood from what has been made, so that men are without excuse."(Romans 1:20) God loves you. God is near to strengthen, care for, and to help. Jesus is the giver and the joy of life. All beyond our five senses, but very very real. You can believe it and trust it today.

DISCOVER GOD

We observed Columbus Day each year. The day recognizes the landing of Christopher Columbus in the Americas in 1492. It also highlights the quest for discovery. The actual record of what the new arrivals did when they got here is quite a mixed bag, but that's a whole other story. What is notable here is that there is something in mankind that drives him to discover. Whether it was the quest by sea to the west centuries ago, or our current desire to explore Mars, we are driven to discovery. One of the fairly recent Nobel winners received the prize for a microscope technique that allows observation down to the molecular level. What does all of this say about us? I think it is another of the many marks of being created by God and for God. Scripture calls us to use that drive to understand and know more about our God. We might also say that, because of sin, we are separated from God, and are seeking to discover our way to return. There are other answers, but it does leave us something to ponder as we think about who we are and who God created us to be. Even further, how do we use this drive to draw us closer to Him and bring honor to His name?

OUR TRUE SHELTER

Little kids love to play in boxes. Put a cardboard box on the floor and watch a child climb in. Adults like shelters, too. We build gazebos, and screened porches. We set up canopy tents in the yard. There is something secure about being under a shelter. The Apostle Paul wrote to the Colossians. "Set your minds on the things above, not on earthly things. For you have died, and your life is now hidden with Christ in God." (Colossians 3:2-3) The word "hidden" means to cover or to shelter. Is the desire we have for a physical shelter pointing us, in a small way, to the ultimate shelter we have in Jesus Christ? Paul points us in the right direction. "Set your minds on the things above." God is our true source of wisdom. His Holy Word is our guide in all matters of faith and life. Further, he says "you have died" pointing to our baptism, that our old nature has died with Christ, and we have been raised to a new life in Him. What better shelter could we have? Far better than a cardboard box. Far more secure than anything this world has to offer.

God Can Be Forgetful Too

As we get older, many of us face the problem of forgetfulness. Did you ever walk into the middle of a room, and then ask yourself, "what did I come in here for?" Come to think of it, I've been doing that for a long time! Did you ever think of God as being forgetful? He is, but His forgetfulness is by choice, and it is selective. In His great mercy He chooses to forget our sins, and not hold them against us. He said through Jeremiah, "I will forgive their wickedness and will remember their sins no more." (Jeremiah 31:34) This is the marvelous forgetfulness of God! As we come to Him by way of the cross of Jesus Christ, He lets all of our sins fall to the ground right there, and sees us wearing the white robe of Christ's righteousness. He remembers our sins no more. So, when we have those "senior moments" it reminds us of the wonderful grace that allows us to walk free with our Lord.

Allowing Them To Struggle

I mentioned last week about how one phrase or one verse of Scripture can stand out as an important truth. Such is the case with a Gospel lesson in Mark 6:48. Jesus had just fed the 5000 on the hillside. He stayed behind to pray while the disciples were out on the lake in their fishing boat. A storm came up. They were struggling at the oars to make some progress to the other side. Jesus came walking on the water, but the text says, "He intended to pass by them". It doesn't say that they were in danger of perishing as in the other storm account. They were struggling, and Jesus intended to pass by. What? Didn't He care? He had just proven He care by feeding the multitude. Now He lets His own disciples struggle. Yes, as we have often done with our own children. We watch over them, but we don't keep them from every difficult task they face in life. We all struggle and grow with the trials we go through. The disciples would later face far more serious trials than rowing against a Galilean wind. This doesn't explain all the trials we face in life, or the times our prayers seem to go unanswered, but it does give us something to ponder. And the Lord did finally calm the winds. Whether we always see it just when we expect or not, the Lord's compassion is always there.

No Disclaimer With God

God's promises do not come with disclaimers. I get very tired of pill commercial on TV. They all come across with great promises for a cure of this and that disease, but they follow by saying that it could leave you in a worse condition, or even kill you. I heard an investment offer on radio a few days ago for a 20% return on your investment with monthly payouts. It was then followed by someone talking at triple speed giving all the conditions and lack of guarantees. Our Lord doesn't work that way. "The LORD is trustworthy in all he promises and faithful in all he does" the psalmist tells us. (Psalm 145:13) As we look back over our lives we see Lord's hand of grace in so many large and small ways. We struggle at times with not seeing immediate answers to prayers we think are right, but we can't deny the goodness He has shown throughout life. The love of our Lord is very great and doesn't come to us disclaimers.

WHAT IS TRUE PROGRESS?

I am old enough to have grown up without a TV in the house, and I really do know how to use a dial telephone. We even had a party line for a while. Even though I was involved with electronics for a number of years I still find the change in modern technology rather astounding. We are enjoying a weeks vacation in a rented cottage in Western Maryland. There is a basket on the coffee table with four remote controls in it. I can barely manage to turn the TV on and off. I sat on the deck this afternoon with an inexpensive smart phone in my hand. In a matter of a minutes I had contacted one daughter in Virginia, and another in Pennsylvania. These great technological advances have improved many things in life. Yet in spite of this, it is progress in a very limited sense. True progress is only that which changes the heart. The inner nature of mankind has really not changed in thousands of years. We struggle with the same sins as did our ancestors. it is only the grace of our Lord working through His Spirit that can touch and change our deepest need. Cell phones and remotes are nice, but life truly progresses through faith in Jesus Christ.

Keep Our Eyes On The Greatest Gift

Everyone likes to get gifts, free stuff, huge discounts, or even win the lottery. But the thing we find with most such gifts is that they are short lived. Many gifts get put aside, free stuff is not all that useful, and many big lottery winners have found the money more of a curse than a blessing. The writer of the Book of James tells us that "Every good and perfect gift is from above, coming down from the Father of the heavenly lights, who does not change like shifting shadows."(James 1:17) We often seek after toys and baubles in life ignoring the One from whom our true treasure comes. It is the Lord who is the source of life. It is He who has given us life in Jesus Christ. God shows us in His Word the path to the best life possible. It is He who loves us with an everlasting love that never changes. Everything else we have in this world can be seen as a gift of God, and received with thankfulness and praise. Sure, getting gifts is nice, but we live daily in the joy of having already received the greatest gift possible, a relationship with Almighty God through faith in Jesus Christ. Everything else flows from this.

Be Careful About Going Along

My home state, Maryland, is in the middle of the eastern seaboard. We have our expressions that are peculiar to our area, but we don't have a real "southern accent" as you might find in states further south in the country. What is interesting, however is how easily one can pick up and begin to mimic the speech of another area when one is living there for a length of time. It is easy to go along. We've also heard the expressions of swearing like a sailor, or a certain kind of talk that goes on in a locker room. I said it is easy to go along, but we do need to be careful what we go along with. Paul wrote to the Colossian Church we should put aside all "anger, wrath, malice, slander, and abusive speech from your mouth."(Colossians 3:8) "Let your speech always be with grace,..."(Colossians 4:6) That doesn't mean we are always talking about religious things. There is a lot of good speech and clean humorous things to laugh about. Our words are to be useful to others, and bring no shame to ourselves or to our Lord.

YES, YOU!

The writer of the Book of Hebrews began his third chapter saying, "Therefore, holy brethren, partakers of a heavenly calling,..." Holy brethren...partakers of a heavenly calling really? We are tempted to say, "Who me?" Paul would write to the churches and begin by calling the people "saints". I don't think these are terms we would usually apply to ourselves. Nor do we often feel like holy brethren. But that is not the point of these expressions. Ephesians 2:8 says "For it is by grace you have been saved, through faith-and this is not from yourselves, it is the gift of God." By God's pure grace we have a heavenly calling. You have been called by God to be His child through faith in Jesus Christ. It is our identity in Jesus. When one has a calling, whether as a Christian Pastor, or as a business professional, or a shop keeper, we seek to fulfill that calling as best God gives us the grace, understanding, and strength to do. So, dear holy brethren, seek to live your calling today to the glory of God.

OUR CALLING

St. Peter writes in his first letter that in view of the life we are being called to we should "prepare (our) minds for action,..."[(1 Peter 1:13)] The literal phrase is to gird up the loins of your mind (as in the King James version). This is an interesting expression. It means to "prepare oneself to face or contend with something. It was used for preparing for hard work, and even for battle. Peter is using it here with reference to our minds, our thoughts. It may seem a strange expression, but it is very real guidance for life. Peter recognized that all sin starts in the mind. Whether, anger, coveting, lust, or whatever. One allows the mind to play with thoughts and desires that are not good. God had said to Cain before his jealousy caused him to kill his brother, "sin is crouching at the door; and its desire is for you, but you must master it."[(Genesis 4:7)] This is the same battle Peter is talking about. I think it is a battle we all experience, and I suspect have often given in too. Peter advises that we above all keep our minds fixed on the greatness of our calling to be in eternal fellowship with our Lord Jesus Christ. As Peter says, a life so great that even angels long to understand it.

TOO GREAT A SACRIFICE

The news media has reported on so many scandals concerning people in high positions. It really seems somewhat strange to me. An intelligent person spends years accomplishing a variety of good things, of having a good marriage and family, having a solid reputation in the community, and then in order to gain some additional wealth, influence, sexual gratification or whatever does something stupid to tarnish everything that has gone before. I know we humans are more complex than that, and our motivations are many, including the sin that resides in the hearts of us all. Yet, it seems that a good reputation and respect of others should be too great a sacrifice to make for the temporary gains one may find. Choices in life are hard. Temptations are many, but maybe weighing the costs can be helpful. In order to gain this, what do I have to give up? It is a question that can be applied to the purchase of that next greatest gadget, or a desired sexual encounter. But even beyond this, as people of faith in the One who gave His life that we might live, the cost of bringing shame to Him is far too great compared to any sinful pleasures.

"I misspoke." Really?

I was reading a magazine the other day where, in different places, the publisher had to make corrections concerning a previous issue. It read "we miss characterized" a particular incident they reported. In another place "we misstated" certain information. We are also familiar with hearing a politician backtrack on some statement saying "I misspoke". It would have been more truthful to say, "we were wrong", "we stated falsely", or how about "I lied". Unmarried couples don't just sleep together, they commit fornication. People don't just have a little too much to drink, they get drunk. We love self justification. It sounds so much better, and after all "nobody's perfect". The problem is that truth is not so easily removed. However it looks on the surface it's still flat out wrong. It is why we in the Christian Church emphasize the importance of confession and absolution. The only true cleansing, the only true freedom, is coming before the Lord, against whom all sin is committed, and honestly repent. Confess our sins, without color or self justification. It is then we can hear the words of forgiveness and cleansing in the atoning sacrifice of Jesus Christ. Even if we have to bear the consequences of our sin, we are free. That's so much better that trying to cover it over, and still bear the guilt.

We Are In A Spiritual Warfare

In some Christian denominations hymns about war and fighting have been removed from their hymnals, or at least verses modified. Hymns like Onward Christian Soldiers, The Battle Hymn of the Republic, or Sons of God Go Forth To War are no longer in favor. No one likes war, and we should all desire and prayer for peace, but we must recognize the real struggle we all face - the battle with the world, with our own sinful flesh, and with the devil. This is a real conflict, a real battle, and is expressed in some of our hymns. Paul counseled the Ephesians Christians to "be strong in the Lord and in his mighty power. Put on the full armor of God,... (Ephesians 6:10-11) This is first a battle within our own hearts to overcome "the sin that so easily entangles us". (Hebrews 12 :1) It is a battle we cannot fight alone. We stand in the light of Christ who "loved us and gave himself up for us", and by the strength of God's Spirit working in our lives. Christ has won the victory at the cross. We live and stand firm daily in the light of that victory.

THOSE WHO COME EMPTY

Jesus always does things backwards! He talked to the Pharisees, respected scholars of their day, and called them hypocrites, and empty tombs. He said if your want to be a leader, you need to be the servant of all. To be first you have to be last. He just didn't get it. And the disciples He chose. Not an important, well educated man among them. He didn't understand about power and prominence in this world. Or maybe He did. Maybe He really saw how hollow and superficial all the things we hold up as goals to strive for really are. Maybe that is why He spent His time with the tax collectors and sinners. There was no pretense in them. They knew they were weak and needed His help. And they received it. The ones who come to Him empty are sure to be filled with His living water.

Not A Museum Relic

One of the newest museums in Washington, D.C. is the Museum of the Bible. I've heard some good reports from people who have gone. There are many interesting and interactive exhibits about how we got the texts of Scripture we use today. There is just one thing that strikes me - the coupling of the two words Museum and Bible. I'm afraid too many people treat the Bible as a museum relic. It is the most published book in the world, but statistics have shown knowledge of the Bible is terrible low. Far from being a museum relic, the Bible is God's holy and revealed word to mankind. Almighty God speaking to us. One would think we would hunger and thirst to understand what God is saying, even as some of the verses themselves say. If you have an opportunity to be in D.C. go visit the Museum of the Bible. But above all use your Bibles. Read, study, meditate upon God's Holy Word. It really is you food for life.

A Treasure In Earthen Vessels

I have an acquaintance I see fairly regularly. We've had a number of good conversations about things of the Lord. He is a man who was hurt by the church years ago and has not returned. Yet he is a believer who reads the Bible and prays daily. I think he is a man of sincere faith, but he is also missing something. It is tragically true that the church has hurt people and driven some away. For this, we in the church, are called to repent. Even so that does not negate the validity and the need for what remains. There are churches where the Word of God is rightly preached and the sacraments rightly administered. Paul said we have this treasure in jars of clay.[(II Corinthians 4:7)] Churches have people in them, and so are flawed, but the treasure is real. We need to hear the Gospel preached, and come to the altar rail to receive the bread and wine with the words "given and shed for you for the forgiveness of your sins". In the midst of the clay jars these are life giving truths that we all need.

AND GOD LAUGHS

We have a couple of dish towels folded over the handle of the oven. Our 3 year old grandson and 2 year old granddaughter love to take them, tuck them in the collar of their shirt like a cape, and run through the house shouting "superman","supergirl". We all laugh. We know it is all play. We know they have no superpowers (except the love they hold over our hearts). Otherwise they are totally dependent upon us. Did you ever think of God laughing? In Psalm 2 God looks at the nations and rulers of the earth and asks, "Why do the nations conspire and the peoples plot in vain? The kings of the earth rise up and the rulers band together against the LORD and against his anointed,..." And then the Psalmist writes, "The One enthroned in heaven laughs; the Lord scoffs at them."[Psalm 2:2-4] It all sounds like a pretty apt picture of today's front page news. The nations in their posturing look much like my two grandkids running through the living room. Unfortunately, it is a lot more serious than that. Yet, our Lord will always have the last laugh. He admonishes them, "Therefore, you kings, be wise; be warned, you rulers of the earth. Serve the LORD with fear and celebrate his rule with trembling."[Psalm 2:10-11] Oh, that they would hear and obey!

PRAY FOR THEM

I have mentioned before about my concern for our young people. I am older and really can't relate to this younger generation, but I can and do pray earnestly for them. I ask you to do the same. Our young people face challenges, temptations, a culture, and opportunities that many of us could never even imagine. I pray for each of our ten grandchildren that the Lord would put a hedge of protection around them. That by His Spirit He would help them make a strong confession of faith in our Lord Jesus. He is still the only source of life as He said in John 5:26. In the midst of trials we face, regardless of age, He is still the right source of wisdom and strength. He is the One who makes our life valuable and gives value to what we do. One day Jesus asked the disciples, "who do you say that I am?". Peter responded "You are the Christ, the Son of the living God". Pray that they, and we, hold firmly to that confession. It is life itself.

No "Little White Lie"

Some years ago I was working on cabinets in a customers kitchen. The mother answered the telephone. It was a friend for the daughter, but for some reason the daughter didn't want to talk with her. She signaled to her mother, and the mother quickly told the friend that the daughter wasn't home. An obvious lie. But how accustomed we have become to playing loose and free with the truth. We are hearing it daily in the news. Lies, half truths, graft, corruption have become a way of life for many. It has ruined many lives, and caused the poverty and starvation of countless thousands in third world countries. Telling a friend a daughter isn't home is no big deal, is it? Yes it is. It is no different from all the corrupt politics we hear of today. The lie is used to save face, to get out of an awkward situation, to gain or maintain power. When the disciples were vying for the top spots in the Kingdom, Jesus said that was the way the world operated, but that "it shall not be so among you."(Matthew 20:26) We deplore much of what goes on in the political realm, but let's be sure we don't contribute to it, even in small ways. We are people who live by the truth, and seek to proclaim it in words and actions.

A Precious Gift

All Saints Day in the Christian calendar is a day we remember all those who have gone on into the presence of our Lord as well as all those alive in the Church today. We are one company together, the communion of saints. This is a bond of fellowship of all those in Jesus Christ, a fellowship that not even death can break. I had the privilege last evening of sharing worship and the Holy Eucharist with forty or so of my brothers and sisters in Christ on the campus of Concordia Theological Seminary in St. Louis, MO. We are a diverse group of people spread across the country, but we came together as one, knelt at the altar and heard the words "given and shed for you for the forgiveness of your sins". What a blessing! What a joy! It is the blessing and joy you also have awaiting you this coming Sunday or whenever you share at the Lord's altar. Don't neglect the meeting together. You need to be there. You need to share this bond of fellowship that Christ so readily extends to you. It is at the Lord's altar that all differences are set aside, and all sins washed away. Leave that place of renewal, as I did last evening, in a depth of joy that only Jesus can supply. Celebrate our Lord dear saint.

Part Of A Great Company Of Believers

"Therefore, since we are surrounded by such a great cloud of witnesses,..." The writer of the Book of Hebrews has just looked back over thousands of years of their history pointing to person after person who stood firm in their faith in spite of fears, doubts, and opposition. That is the cloud of witnesses he is referring to in chapter 12. Sometimes we feel like we are lone Christians in our own world. There are times in the solitude of the night our fears and doubts play havoc with our thoughts. But we are not alone. We are truly a part of many who have gone before us who have struggled just as we are and more. They have come through. God has proved faithful, and will prove faithful to us. "Let us throw off everything that hinders and the sin that so easily entangles. And let us run with perseverance the race marked out for us, fixing our eyes on Jesus, the pioneer and perfecter of faith." (Hebrews 12:.1&2) Be encouraged dear Christian. Jesus is alive, and leading the way.

True Value

What really is of value? A recent report tells of a rare Revolutionary War penny that sold for over one million dollars. I understand its rarity, and historic value, but more than a million? That is only a small example of how values today have gotten warped out of shape. We could look at sports and entertainment salaries, and a variety of other things. I don't begrudge anyone what they have. Nor do I envy any others. The Lord has been so very gracious with us. Nor are we going to change very much of the value structure of this world, but we should ask the question I began with, what really is of value? What really is lasting, that can never be take from us? Possessions and jobs can be lost, even health which we greatly prize, but our relationship with Christ will last for eternity. And those we hold dear in our heart, even beyond death. These alone are lasting, and worthy of our greatest efforts. We need all of the things that sustain physical life, and also give pleasure, but we remind ourselves that these are not the things of true value in life.

God's Workmanship

Do you like to make things? It can be anything from a craft, to a good meal, to a house. When we make something we have a plan for it. We work progressively stage by stage. We have an anticipation about its completion and how it will be used. And when it is completed we can enjoy it and take pride in it. Did you ever think of applying this process to your own life? This morning I read part of a prayer from Psalm 138, "your love, LORD, endures forever-- do not abandon the works of your hands."(Psalm 138:8) "The work of you hand." That started me thinking about how many verses speak of us, you and me, as God's handiwork. "For we are God's handiwork, created in Christ Jesus to do good works..."(Ephesians 2:10) We all struggle at times with our direction in life, decisions we must make, our own temptations and sins, and many other things that occupy our days. Life is not easy, but neither is the saw blade that cuts the wood that will fit into a useful piece of furniture. We can't see the completed project, but we can trust the master builder who is continually working in it all. "He who began a good work in you will carry it on to completion until the day of Christ Jesus."(Philippians 1:6)

Expressions Of God's Love

A man came to Jesus one day and asked, Teacher, which is the greatest commandment of the Law? Jesus replied: "'Love the Lord your God with all your heart and with all your soul and with all your mind and with all your strength."(Matthew 22:37) Yesterday I asked for thoughts about my tin can telephone. I received a number of thoughtful replies. You see, when we look around in life we see the gracious hand of God in so many, and sometimes very unexpected, places. Too often people only see the bad stuff our sin has caused in the world and ask "if God is a loving God how could He allow.....? But they miss the many demonstrations of God's grace around each day. It is His hand even in such mundane things as tin can telephones that shows us His love, and causes us to turn to Him again in love. Dear Christian friend God loves you personally and deeply. He is working in your life in so many ways. He has demonstrated "his own love for us in this: While we were still sinners, Christ died for us. (Romans 5:8) There has been no greater expression of God's love than what we see in Jesus. Keep Him at the center of your life and return His love with heart, soul, mind, and strength.

Jesus' Work In Us

Peter, John, and a few other disciples were with Jesus on the shore of the Sea of Galilee after His resurrection. Jesus took Peter aside to talk with him. John was not far away. After some necessary conversation between the two Peter looked back at John and said, "Lord, what about this man?". Jesus responded, "If I have a different plan for his life what is that to you?". Peter, Jesus was saying, You will have enough to deal with if you pay attention to the conduct of your own life. A good lesson for our age and any age. We are sinful people living in a broken world. We worry a lot about this one or that one not doing what they should, or what we would like them to do. But we can't change them. We can only change ourselves. We pray for other. We minister and help in whatever situations we are able. But our prayer is for the Lord Jesus to continue to change and guide our own lives that we may be able to love and serve other in a better way. Read the John 21 account. That's what Jesus was doing with Peter so that he became an effective servant to the Jewish community and to the newly born Christian Church.

OUR MEANING

Why do we continue writing, speaking, teaching, and preaching about Jesus? Psalm 100 expresses it this way, "For the LORD is good and his love endures forever; his faithfulness continues through all generations." [Psalm 100:5] We desire to extend that good to all people. Our Lord is the source of life. We want all to find life in Him. Jesus is not just a nice add-on to an already good life. He is life itself. He said, "I am the way, the truth, and the life." [John 14:6] He is not just the back up plan if all else fails. He is the plan and purpose for life, the one who gives life its meaning. "Worship the LORD with gladness; come before him with joyful songs." [Psalm 100:2] As we come to Him with worship and praise we find strength, life, and peace.

EVEN A SCIENTIFIC STUDY

Jesus told us that we "ought always to pray and not lose heart".[(Luke 18:1)] Scientific studies have been done on prayer - with two control groups, etc. etc. It did show that the group prayed for did measurably better than the other. But then Jesus has been telling us that all the time. How dull and slow we are to learn! Our God does hear and care. He does respond. There is nothing we cannot take before Him. He desires and is working for our best good. Do pray, and not lose heart.

One Thing That Never Grows Old

The next new thing has a real appeal. A new gadget comes out and people line up at the stores to get theirs. Even the next big entertainer draws massive crowds and is in the tabloid papers. But something we learn fairly quickly is that the new grows old. It has been surpassed, replaced by a better model. That once fantastic item gets put aside and forgotten. (How many old cell phones do you have sitting on a shelf somewhere?) When Israel came out of Egypt they were given manna to eat during their desert wanderings. It was renewed every morning. They couldn't hoard it for another day. They had to trust God for each day's provision, and they were always filled. In the midst of one of Israel's most difficult times the Prophet Jeremiah writes, "The LORD'S lovingkindness indeed never ceases, For His compassion never fail. They are new every morning; Great is Your faithfulness." (Lamentations 3:22-23) Oh, we will continue to look for the new stuff that the world puts out, but what we really need never fails, never wears out, never grows old. God's grace and loving kindness is there for free every morning.

A True Father

In the book of James the writer says, "The Lord is full of compassion and mercy. "(James 5:11) That is true and many verses in Scripture speak of the grace and love of God. But at the same time God is not a pushover. He is a Father. Our problem is that we have lost the true concept of a man and of good father. He is not self indulgent. A father gives of himself sacrificially for the good of his wife and children. At the same time he is firm in the moral and spiritual direction the family is to go. He is a protector, but he is also willing to let his children struggle with difficult tasks, and take some hard knocks. He prays continually for his family that the Lord would protect them physically and spiritually, and that their hearts would be opened more and more to the Lord. If we begin to understand a bit more of the Scriptural picture of man, and of a good father, we will understand more of the nature of our God.

Our Confession

There is an ancient practice that has been in the Church since the beginning, the practice of confession and absolution. We begin each of our worship services with this practice to prepare ourselves to come before our holy God and to receive the body and blood of Christ in the Eucharist. We kneel before the altar and confess "I have sinned against You in my thoughts, with my words, and in my actions." Do we really believe that? Can we be that honest with God, or do we just mouth the words? We are coming before our God of perfect and total love, but also our God who is brilliant and burning holiness. His love longs to cleanse and restore us to life, but the light of His holiness requires that we humble ourselves, put aside all pretenses, all excuses, all self justifications. We can't enumerate each and ever sin. We don't need to. We simply bow humbly in our guilt and ask for His mercy. It is then that we can hear the cleansing and forgiving words of life in Jesus Christ. The memories and consequences of sin remain, but they lose their power to destroy our lives. We are free to begin again in His holiness.

Moral Character Matters

Proverbs 14:34 says "Righteousness exalts a nation, But sin is a disgrace to any people." Character in leadership makes a difference. This is true whether in the fields of politics, religion, sports, or media. People in leadership become examples that others look up to. There moral character matters along with their competence in the work they do. Unfortunately, our society has been more and more able to separate the two, and give excuses for poor moral character. We love the phrase, "nobody's perfect", or "we're all sinners". That seems to excuse whatever we want to do, or accept in others. Of course it is true. No one is perfect. We all sin. But Scripture always holds leaders to a higher standard. A people need leaders they can look up to rather than excuse. The Bible certainly shows its share of leaders who had great faults, but the ones God could use were the ones who were willing to repent and turn from their sin rather than justify themselves and continue as if it didn't matter. I'm afraid in too many areas today we are wiling to overlook wrongdoing bringing reproach on our people. It's time for thinking more seriously what righteousness means.

Do That Prayer Thing

A physical therapist my wife sees often is also a dear Christian sister with whom we share prayer requests. She told my wife of an incident in her neighborhood this past week. The mother of a young man who lives across the street was taken to the hospital by ambulance. The young man came over to our friend and asked "if she could do that prayer thing" for his mother. He had some vague concept of a god who some how hears our concerns, but probably likens him to Santa Claus or the Easter Bunny. There is a whole generation of young men and woman with the same background. Dear Christian friends we have work to do. I don't ask you to go stand on a street corner and start preaching. That's not my style either. But the Lord does give us opportunities each day to witness to our life in Jesus Christ. Look for them. Expect them. And be ready to do "that prayer thing" on the spot when it is needed. More will happen in a minute or two of sincere prayer, than many minutes of preaching. Put aside your self consciousness. Don't worry about the right words. The Lord will give them. Let's shine some light in the darkness of this generation.

OUR REASON TO GIVE THANKS

The last Thursday in November has been designated by the U.S. Congress as a day for national Thanksgiving. More than ever this year it seems like Thanksgiving has become submerged with Black Friday sales and very early Christmas decorations. Even so, we need to pause and think about the meaning of this day. There has been a song running through my head the last couple of days that expresses what this day should be for us - Give Thanks written by Don Moen in 1986. Give thanks with a grateful heart:

Give thanks to the Holy One

Give thanks because He's given Jesus Christ, His Son

To give thanks means that we are giving thanks to a person. Who is that? Ourselves for our own strength? Our government for laws and policies they established? Some general benevolent force out there somewhere? Our thanks is only due to One who is above all, who created us and all that is. Above all the family, friends, and material things we have, He has given us the unimaginable gift of Himself in the person of His Son, Jesus Christ. It is in Him that we have life. We can then go on to sing:

And now let the weak say, "I am strong."

Let the poor say, "I am rich

Because of what the Lord has done for us"

Everything in our world is not perfect. There are things we need or would like to see changed. But above all we have a Lord who has chosen to be a part of our lives. In Him we live, and move, and have our being.(Acts 17:28) For that we give the most hearty thank. Do have a very blessed and Thankful Day.

WHAT IS TRULY IMPORTANT

There is something inconsistent with yesterday and today coming together as they do. Yesterday was a day of thanksgiving, a day to focus on all the blessings we have received. Today is the Black Friday sales day where people rush out to get more of the stuff they said they were thankful for yesterday. Each year there are stories about the long lines in front of stores, people waiting to shop long before the store opens. Some people have camped out all night to be the first in line to get the best bargain. Some are willing to sacrifice their comfort, their time, their sleep in order to get something that likely will be obsolete or broken in a few years. We are strange people! Thanksgiving Day yesterday was about something quite different. It was about realizing and remembering all of the sacrifices that have been made for us to have the life we have. Hopefully this also stirs us to be willing to sacrifice something of ourselves for the good of others. I'm not saying that we shouldn't try to get the best deal on something we want to buy, but let's keep our perspective fixed on what is truly important.

GOD IS A REAL PERSON

We teach children the simple table grace, "God is great, God is good, and we thank Him for our food." Simple, maybe even a bit simplistic for adults, but it is also profound. God is great! There is none greater, omnipotent, omniscient, and omnipresent. He is creator of all things. He made us and all that is. He gives us every breath that we take. If He made us He also has shown us the best way in which we can live. God is good! He is a Father, our Father, who always seeks the best for us, and uses all things for our good. He is not just a general force out there somewhere. He is a person who knows and cares about each one of us personally. We could go on for many lines about His greatness and goodness, and we should in our own times of prayer and meditation. Because of all of this, He is due our overwhelming thanks. Not just for food, but for everything that comes to us. Maybe we need to remind ourselves again about the simple things we teach our children. They really are true.

DON'T LOSE THE WONDER

Don't ever lose the wonder! A few weeks ago we were in the office of our orthopedic doctor. On the walls of his examining room were six charts of various parts of the body - the hands, the legs and feet, and so forth. One of them was even called "The Amazing Back". There is such a complexity to the body that even the artists who did the drawings found it amazing. And we know that the body is so complex that we need specialists for each part. I looked at the chart of The Amazing Back and thought, "my God made that". It is the wonder, the majesty, of my God and yours who brought us into being. Even further, He made us with a human spirit which separates us from all others of the animal kingdom. The wonder goes on as we understand that He knows and love each one individually, and has redeemed us by the precious blood of His only begotten Son, Jesus Christ. We are so much more than a chart on the doctors wall. Don't ever lose the wonder, and bow before Him in worship.

CHOICES

Little blue letters on the computer screen - click on them and they will get you today's news and weather, or a Bible passage, or a porn site. Satellite companies advertise that they bring 600 channels of TV into your home. The computer provides a thousand times that and more. In our modern world we are presented with such a vast array of choices that it boggles the mind. It is really a question of what we want. Do we want those things that strengthen our lives, that can serve as good for others, and that draw us closer to our Lord? This is more than deciding on a few clicks of a computer mouse, or TV remote. It is the basic attitude we establish for our lives. When Mary, the sister of Lazareth, sat at Jesus' feet listening to Him, He said of her, "Mary has chosen the best portion, and it will not be taken from her."(Luke10:42) In all the choices that confront us daily, Lord help us to choose the best portion.

Temptations

Jesus told us that "temptations are sure to come". We are all tempted to sin in one way or another. But even the word sin implies that we have been given a standard, a value, that we should not transgress. In a day when society seeks to reject any values as absolute there are still some universally recognized, murder and sexual crimes among them. So it is not so easy to get rid of the word sin. And the fact of sin implies that there is an absolute good (our Lord) against whom all actions are measure. As we are tempted to sin it is always by something we like, something we want, something we desire to gain. In the Genesis account of creation we are told that "the woman saw that the fruit of the tree was good for food, and pleasing to the eye, and also desirable for gaining wisdom..."[(Genesis 3:6)] That is what makes resisting temptation so difficult. It is an internal battle between "I want" and "I know it's wrong". The motivation for resisting temptation, for overcoming the "I want", is that we desire to please and bring honor to the One who is the Good above all.

PEACE IN A BROKEN WORLD

A Hurricane batters the eastern coast of the U.S. There are necessary preparations and evacuations in the Carolinas. There will be a great cost and effort to rebuild after the storm passes. Tragically, some lives may even be lost. Whether natural disasters or trials cause by the sinfulness of man, we are faced with the truth that we live in a fallen world. Yet it is a world into which God has come with His redeeming love. It's hard to see that love in the midst of the storm, but it is there. It is seen in the lives of people who give aid. Ultimately, it will be seen in the fulfilled promise of God making all things new. At one of the most critical and frightening times in the lives of His disciples Jesus said to them, "Peace I leave with you; my peace I give you. I do not give to you as the world gives. Do not let your hearts be troubled and do not be afraid." (John 14:27) We may lose property. We may even lose physical life. But we cannot lose the love of God who will make all things new.

With God All Things Are Possible

Scripture uses a number of forms to convey its truth. Some things are quite literal, other figurative or allegorical. We don't set aside our human reason when we read the Bible, but we do need to be careful how we apply it. I ran across one example, perhaps minor, in Psalm 147 verse 4. "He determines the number of the stars, and calls them all by name". Well now, we know from astronomy that there are billions and billions of stars. We've looked into the heavens and can't even fathom its magnitude. It is not within human reason to know the full number of them, and to give each one a name - really? But this is Almighty God we are talking about. Is it not possible that such a statement is literally true? How about a great fish swallowing a man, or creating the cosmos in six days? Let's be careful how much reason we apply to Scripture. Let the Bible be its own interpreter. We weren't there when creation came into being, nor were we on the boat with Jonah. Our God is a awesome God, and capable of more that we can ever imagine. "Great is our Lord and mighty in power; his understanding has no limit." [Psalm 147:5] Let us bow in worship.

Washed In Baptism

There is a difference between a mirror and a photograph. They both show an image, but a photo can be touched up to make the subject look good. A mirror shows it like it is. At the Tabernacle, the Old Testament Jewish worship center, there was a bronze basin in which the priests would wash before going into the Holy Place of the sanctuary. To make that basin they collected the highly polished bronze mirrors of the ladies, and shaped them into a large bowl. This basin is symbolic of God's Word, the Holy Scriptures. When we read the Bible it shows fallen human life as it is with all of its warts and blemishes. It shows us our own life with all of its failures and sins. While the bronze bowl of God's Word shows us just as we are, it also holds the water for our cleansing. We are washed in the redemptive waters of our baptism, made clean, and able to walk into the presence of God. In Jesus Christ we are made new, not just touched up. God now sees us through the righteousness of Christ. "It is by grace you have been saved, through faith--and this is not from yourselves, it is the gift of God..."(Ephesians 2:8) And we can only bow in humble worship.

JUST AS MUCH TRAINING

Coming into the fall season the baseball pennant race is heating up. The football season is getting under way. Team members are demonstrating how much effort must go into their sport in order to be successful. Each player has spent years of intense work to get where they are today. The same is true for those who achieve success in academics, and other fields. They apply desire, skill, determination, and years of work. These qualities also need to be applied to our "search" for God. When Paul was in Athens he said to the people, that God made man "so that they should seek Him, in the hope that they might grope for Him and find Him, though He is not far from each one of us." (Acts 17:27) To the Philippines he wrote, "I press on to take hold of that for which Christ Jesus took hold of me." (Philippines 3:12) God has first reached out to us. Otherwise we would not even consider Him. God loves us, and is always close at hand, but to truly know Him and understand something of His nature it takes desire, study, discipline, and persistence. He is with us all along the way, and His love draws us more deeply into His life.

Excitement In The Lord's Truth

As Christians we believe that the death and resurrection of Jesus are central to our faith. It is in these sovereign acts of God's grace that we have forgiveness of sins, and a new and eternal life. This is the Gospel, the old old story that has been repeated for many generations. Recently I've been reading a work by a theological professor writing on the meaning of the cross. He brings out a depth of truth I had not thought of before. I have found it exciting to see aspects of God's grace that are deep and wonderful. There is excitement for a new Christian when they realize that in Christ they have been cleansed and made righteous before God. But that's not all. There is an infinite depth in our Lord that can never be exhausted. The excitement continues as the Lord draws us closer to Himself. Continue to read, think, and pray. There is always more grace, truth, and real excitement in walking day by day with Jesus Christ.

Boundaries Are Good

What parent has not been the brunt of a child's anger when they have had to discipline them or deny them of something they wanted to do? The parent is accused of being hateful or of unloving. Or sometimes it's the response, "everyone else is doing it, why can't I?" We know the very opposite is true. The parent is not being hateful or unloving. It is because of love that the parent sets boundaries, and denies certain things that can be harmful. We want the best for them. The same thing is true when we, as Christians, speak out against behaviors and actions that Scripture says are harmful, particularly those involving human sexuality. Many centuries ago King Solomon wrote, "There is a way which seems right to a man, But its end is the way of death. "(Proverbs 14:12) God is our Father. When He has set boundaries for our lives in his Holy Word, He has done it out of love and for our best good. When we uphold those values it is because of His love we desire all people to know.

One Whole Book

A loose leaf Bible! Sounds funny doesn't it? but that is the way many individuals and liberal Christian denominations are treating the Bible. Or to use another illustration, let's think of a book editor. Some years ago I worked with an editor on a book I published. The editor would look at sentences or paragraphs, making changes or suggesting things be removed entirely. I was happy with the final result, but that is not the way we treat the Bible. It is true that the Bible was written by 40 different individuals over a period of 1500 years, but it is one book, all 66 individual chapters. It is a book inspired by God's Spirit and remarkably consistent from Genesis through Revelation. It is a book that reveals the nature of the human heart, and the truth of all God has done to cleanse and redeem those hearts. There are parts that make us uncomfortable because they are speaking to our rebellious nature, but we don't have the right to throw pages away, or edit pages out that we don't like. We take the Bible as one book, and see what God through His Spirit is saying to us.

To Love And Share Jesus

In the past couple of weeks I've had lunch and lengthy conversations with a Baptist pastor, I've taught from material by an Anglican Bishop, and listened to teaching from a Lutheran seminary professor and a Greek Orthodox Priest. Are their differences in our doctrines? Very definitely. But there is also a common and very important factor. We all love the Lord Jesus Christ, and we want others to know and love Him also. Do the differences matter? Yes they do. We are in a broken and confused world and we don't have a single apostolic, prophetic authority as they did at the first church council in Acts 15. As Paul taught, for conscious sake each one must be clear in his own mind.^(Romans 14:5) But we do have the commonality of Holy Scripture and the guidance of God, the Holy Spirit. We must follow God's Word as best we understand it. The single center of that Word is the Lord Jesus Christ, the Word made flesh. Where we gather together around Him, seeking to lift Him up, we can rejoice together beyond our labels as one body in Christ.

POWER OF FORGIVENESS

Forgiveness is a powerful and necessary characteristic for life. In our fallen state we all have our share of self-centeredness, and ignorance of others needs and feelings. This causes us to hurt and be hurt. It causes us to offend both God and others. The power to forgive and be forgiven was gained for us at the cross. It is vital that we depend upon daily. We have no life with God apart from the forgiveness granted us through Christ. We have no relationship with others unless we are willing to forgive, and to ask for forgiveness. Forgiveness has been given to us at the greatest possible cost. Let's be willing to use it wherever it is needed in all of our relationships.

More Than Answers

Questions! Life leaves us with many questions. Why is it this way? What will happen if.....? Why didn't......? Some questions motivate new directions and investigations which lead to very helpful discoveries in a variety of fields. Others seem to hang in the air with no reasonable answer. Those can be really frustrating, especially when in relation to our Lord. It is always interesting in reading the questions asked to Jesus in the Gospels. Most often He didn't answer them directly as the questioner would have liked. Rather, He points to something deeper, something more necessary to be dealt with first. And some questions don't seem to get answered at all. It is those questions that turn us back to truths we already know and believe - that God does love us, that He has given the life of His Son to redeem us, that He cares deeply about all that touches us, that His will is perfect and that He will bring all things to their right conclusion for our good. It is in these truths that all of our questions rest. We pray. We do all we are able, but we live in trust of the One who is our life. We can be at peace even when all our questions don't get answered.

Do Not Be Anxious

I'll pass on something to you that I heard in our worship service this evening at our Pastor's Conference. We know how Google and Amazon track everything we do on their sites. Well, apparently they also track the number of times people underline various verses in electronic Bible texts. We were surprised to learn that the most underlined verse is not John 3:16 or one of the other well know passages. It is Philippians 4:6-7. "Do not be anxious about anything, but in every situation, by prayer and petition, with thanksgiving, present your requests to God. And the peace of God, which transcends all understanding, will guard your hearts and your minds in Christ Jesus." It strikes me that we live in a very anxious world, which is the likely reason for so many underlining these verses. But we all need to take them to heart. Don't be anxious about anything - not easy to follow through. But Paul give his counsel, "in every situation by prayer and petition with thanksgiving" lay it all before our Lord. God is calling us to be at peace in Him, and we can be. Read on through to verse 9. God wants us to be at peace in Him. He has not failed us, and He will not fail us now.

GIVEN A NEW LIFE

I had the privilege a couple of weeks ago of holding a little baby in my arms, leaning over a bowl of water in front of our altar at church, and pouring water on the baby's head three times - in the Name of the Father, and of the Son, and of the Holy Spirit. Something miraculous happened in that simple act. God worked a mighty work in that child's life. He was cleansed and forgiven the sin inherited from our first parents. He was renewed and given a new life in Jesus Christ. And he was delivered from the power of death and the devil. Yes, all that literally happened. That little boy was given a totally new life in Jesus Christ. So were you when you were baptized. It doesn't matter whether you remember it or not. God did that for you in your baptism. St. Paul wrote to the Roman church, "don't you know that all of us who were baptized into Christ Jesus were baptized into his death? We were therefore buried with him through baptism into death in order that, just as Christ was raised from the dead through the glory of the Father, we too may live a new life."(Romans 6:3-4) You were forgiven. You were renewed. You were delivered from death and the power of the devil. You still yield to temptation and sin, but you "have an Advocate with the Father Jesus Christ the Righteous."(I John 2:1) Because of your baptism you can take that sin and lay it at the foot of the cross, receiving again the white robe of Christ's righteousness. "For you died, and your life is now hidden with Christ in God."(Colossians 3:3) What a miracle! Rejoice!

Kingdom Citizens

Christians are people who are living in two worlds. One world is the visible realm we occupy. The other is the, no less real, spiritual realm of God's Kingdom. The Kingdom is mentioned over 125 times in the four Gospels. The preaching of John, Jesus, and all the Apostles began, "Repent, for the Kingdom of Heaven is at hand." With the incarnation of Almighty God in Jesus Christ, the heavenly spiritual realm of God Kingdom broke into this visible physical realm. With the resurrection of Jesus from the dead we have the assurance that these two realms cannot be separated. Each day we go about our normal routine, doing, to the best of our ability, all the earthly things the day requires. But our strength, our endurance, our desire to live and serve, our very life, comes from the unseen and spiritual realm of God's Kingdom. We are citizens of that Kingdom now, each day and every day.^(Philippians 3:20) That is who you are, dear Christian. Know that your are walking in the light of Christ's Kingdom today.

More Than My Feelings

How easy it is to be manipulated by emotions. Political candidates use catch words like children, or the elderly. Higher taxes, and the rich are also good for a vote or two. TV commercials guarantee to make us thinner or more beautiful, declaring that "we're worth it". Emotions are fine. God gave them to us, and they have their place, but they are not to direct the course of life. Paul wrote to the Philippians, "Do nothing out of selfish ambition or vain conceit. Rather, in humility value others above yourselves, not looking to your own interests but each of you to the interests of the others."(Philippians 2:3-4) Emotional responses are concerned with what is good for me, and for my group. It narrows our focus to what we think is good, but denies the possibility of making hard choices that may require suffering, but in the long run bring real good for all. Read the rest of the Philippian passage, vss.5-8, and consider where we would be if Jesus had acted on emotion rather than the truth of God's purpose for mankind. "Therefore be alert and of sober mind so that you may pray."(I Peter 4:7)

OUR FIRST LOVE

At the beginning of Revelation chapter two the Lord commended the church of Ephesus for a number of things, but said that He had one things against them, they had "forsaken their first love", or "the love they had at first". This didn't mean that they weren't holding to the true faith, or weren't caring for people. They were doing both. What had grown dull was their pure love for Jesus, and their desire to know Him deeply and have Him physically present with them. Above all of our right doctrines and sincere loving service to others is our desire to know and be with our Lord. Jesus is our Bridegroom. Our only natural and fulfilling place is with Him. As time had gone on in the first Christian century and Jesus had not returned the longing for Him had grown dull. I'm afraid it has also with many of us. We continue to teach, share His truth, and serve in His name as God gives us the strength and grace to do, but our desire, our longing, is for His presence alone. All else flows from this.

Peace Now

For time saving devices they sure take up a lot of time. I was on the computer. I had a phone call on the land line, and was handling a text message at the same time. Which takes priority? Which do I do first? True, I'm not going to give up any of the devices, but juggling one's life around them and the other demands of life can be a challenge. Jesus said to His disciples, "Peace I leave with you. My peace I give unto you. I do not give to you as the world gives."(John 14:27) Sometimes we wonder where is that peace? But it really is there. There is a Bible song we often sing called "Jesus is the rock of my salvation". A simple song but a real truth. Jesus is the rock, our solid rock, in the midst of life. Things in life are not likely to get any less complicated, but we do have a solid rock on which to hold. Jesus is our peace.

Not Just An Attachment

When we send an e-mail we can add an attachment. It is usually something that is interesting or helpful. It's easy to do. A few clicks of the mouse and a document or a picture is added to the e-mail. Our problems in life come when we treat God as an attachment. Many see God as interesting or helpful in certain situations, but otherwise off to the side and relatively unimportant to the task of getting along in life. But our God, revealed to us in Jesus Christ, must not be treated that way. Scripture, both Old and New Testaments picture man's relationship with God as that of the bride to the bridegroom. No bridegroom, no spouse, ever wants to be treated as an attachment. Our God calls us to be His bride. He knows us deeply, and has declared that He will never leave of forsake us. Our God cares about every situation, every choice, every action of life - of our lives, as one spouse cares for another. He will not be just an attachment. The more we understand God in the depth of the relationship He calls us to, the more we want to be a part of Him, and have Him a part of all we are and all we do.

DRAW YOUR STRENGTH FROM OUR LORD

A friend of mine who is a serious woodworker used to say that when he felt down or depressed it was time to go buy another woodworking tool. That always picked up his spirits. Well, I'm not sure that's the best remedy, and it certainly is only temporary. We all have times of feeling down. It is often a matter of the direction in which our eyes are looking. Are we looking only at the problems, or to the One who is greater than all we might face. Take some time today and read Isaiah 40, especially vss. 21- 31. "Do you not know? Have you not heard? ... Have you not understood since the earth was founded? He sits enthroned above the circle of the earth. ... To whom will you compare me? Or who is my equal?" says the Holy One. Lift your eyes and look to the heavens: Who created all these? ... Do you not know? Have you not heard? The LORD is the everlasting God, the Creator of the ends of the earth. He will not grow tired or weary, and his understanding no one can fathom. He gives strength to the weary and increases the power of the weak. Even youths grow tired and weary, and young men stumble and fall; but those who hope in the LORD will renew their strength." Draw your strength from the Lord today.

THOU SHALL NOT .....

Listening to the news often gives one a number of things to ponder. We've been hearing a lot about investigations taking place in Washington. One of the lawyers in the national level corruption case said that the defendant had not been given a warning that it was a felony to lie to an FBI investigator taking his statement. Really? A warning not to lie? I was under the impression that Moses had given that warning 3500 years ago. "Thou shall not bear false witness." The term fake news has been coined today. That is simply media lying. I know I am idealistic, and would like to think that everyone knows that "truth is the best policy". But honestly, when you hear a statement from someone in authority saying that one needs a warning the lying is wrong we are in sad shape. But then we are in sad shape. It is called sin. Whether we like the word or not it is the corruption that infects every one of us. And that is the reason God came among us in Jesus, the Redeemer.

A Weak God In The Straw

The focus of many greeting cards this time of year is the nativity scene. Some churches around our way will have a live nativity with real people and animals. Some try to recreate a Bethlehem village seeking to give the feel of that first Christmas day. We sing carols about sweet baby Jesus meek and mild. But what is it that we are trying to recreate, and who is it sleeping in the straw fill animal feeding trough? When one looks into that manger they are seeing God. God come in all the weakness and vulnerability of an infant. They are seeing God come into the midst of all the smells, pains, and trials of human life. They are seeing God who, out of love for all the people He created, chose to humble Himself and share every aspect of the good and the bad we face in this broken world. Looking into that roughhewn makeshift crib they are seeing - we are seeing - God who came to redeem us from the power of sin, death, and the devil. "For unto you is born this day in the city of David a Saviour who is Christ the Lord." And we like those humble Judean shepherds before us kneel at that manger and worship.

FOR MORE THAN
A TAX DEDUCTION

We've all gotten those letters seeking year end donations. Also, many e-mail from a variety of organizations. The U.S. our tax code allows us to take charitable deduction from our income for tax purposes. So it is a savings, and I think many of us take advantage of it as we should. There have been rumors at times about changes to the tax codes not allowing this or at least modifying it. But I've also thought about the motivation for our giving. Are we committed enough to a particular cause that we would support it even if we were not allowed the deduction? I would hope the answer is yes. Giving should be a matter of true concern for the continuation and growth of organizations we believe are doing good work for the well being of others, and not just because we receive some benefit from it. I will continue to use this deduction because our laws allow it, but my true concern is for the good I believe those dollars will do, and that remains no matter what the calendar date.

Love Came In The Midst Of Life

I started my day by writing a list of what I would like to get done today. I don't always do that, but this is a busy time of year and we all have things we would like to accomplish before Christmas. But Christmas will come whether they all get done exactly as we would like or not. The great truth of God's grace is that God came into human life as it is, and not as we would like it to be. Mary and Joseph weren't prepared to have a baby in a smelly barn. The shepherds didn't get a chance to change their clothe before being surrounded by a host of God's angels. Life is messy. We are sinful. Our great plans don't always work. But God came anyway. He didn't wait for us to clean up our act, and get all things in order. He came to love us in the midst of the disorder and sin of life, to share it all with us, and to show us the way into the fullness of His life. I hope I get my list completed. I hope you get your's done, but it doesn't really matter. Things can wait. His love is always present and guiding us in all our needs.

The True Reason For The Season

The Advent Season prepares us for Christmas and the celebration of the birth of our Lord. It also looks forward to His promised return. There are a number of teachings taken from different passages of Scripture about how Jesus will return and what He will do. Many of us believe that He return is near, but the truth from Scripture is that we can't know when Jesus will come again. That is something only God, the Father, knows. And we don't know exactly what it will look like when He does come. We are taught to watch, to be aware of our times, and be prepared. We should want and long for the soon return of our Lord. That longing is not just for Him to take us out of this evil world. Rather, as both Old and New Testaments say, He is our Bridegroom. We, the Church, are His Bride. The longing of a bride is always to be with her groom. The Lord will deal with each one according to His perfect justice, but our desire is to draw as many into His love as possible so that we may all be joined to Him at His return.

THE GREATEST GIFT

Our daughter teaches first grade at a local elementary school. I asked her how the kids were doing in this week before Christmas. She said they were pretty much off the wall with excitement which make getting their attention a little difficult for lessons. But maybe we should take a lessons from them. Should we not get excited about Jesus? Oh, I know, there is a lot to do to get ready for "the day". Gifts to buy, cards to send out, dinners to plan, visits to prepare for. All of that is nice and important, and yes, we know that "Jesus is the reason for the season". But the more we think about what God has done for us in Jesus Christ - the depth of love He has for the world that caused Him to come among us Himself; His plan of redemption to take punishment we deserve and give us the perfect righteous of His Son; the gift of forgiveness, new life, hope, and strength that we share in His presence each day. Are these not gifts far surpassing any package placed under the Christmas tree? The little ones don't understand this yet. It is ours to show them that the love we share in material gifts can only come from the far greater love we have all been given in the Gift wrapped in clothes and lying in a bed of straw. And that is exciting!

An Electric S'mores Maker! Really?

My family asked me to give them a list of things I would like for Christmas. I always have a problem with this because I really don't need anything. There is nothing I particularly want. But I did make the effort Sunday. I looked through all the volume of advertisements that came with the Sunday paper to see if there was anything that struck my fancy. Well, a couple of things came up as possibilities, but one item caught my attention for a Good Morning comment. For $28 one can buy an "electric s'mores maker". I read that and thought "that's just sad"! Now a s'mores is one of those gummy concoctions made with gram crackers, melted marshmallow, and a piece of chocolate bar. They are wonderful. But they are intended to be made while sitting around a campfire in the evening, roasting marshmallow on the end of a stick, blowing out the flame when it catches on fire, and quickly putting it between two crackers with a piece of chocolate. All the while laughing and talking with friends and family. Maybe even singing a few songs. Must we really mechanize everything? Might we not consider making time for some of the older slower ways of doing some things that involved people, and conversation. Maybe even a family camping trip on the living room floor around the fireplace. Seems to me that that might be better than a $28 electric s'mores maker. Which, by the way, is not on my list. Give it some thought.

GOD FULFILLS HIS PROMISES

God has not been silent. Through many centuries, through many individuals, He told of the coming redemption to be brought by His Son. He has fulfilled all of the words spoken by the prophets concerning the coming and the life of Jesus. He has further promised that Jesus will return to conclude His good purpose for creation. God has not been silent through all the centuries since the birth of our Lord. He has spoken through His Holy Word, and through the circumstances of life by the presence of His Spirit. God has shown Himself to be a God who is present with His people and not one far off. We do not know all that is ahead, or all that is in the plan of God, but a God, our God, who has let His voice be heard throughout all human history is a God of love who can be trusted for each of the days ahead.

The Manger And The Cross

We took a ride last evening to our son and daughter-in-law's home about 50 miles away. In this season many of the homes are lighted in brightly colored decorations, and also a number of those inflatable lawn figures of Santa, Disney characters, and others. We even saw a blow up dog - I think it was supposed to be a dog - that had to be taller than I am. There were a number of manger scenes reminding those passing by of the wonderful birth we are celebrating. It was also interesting to see a number of homes that included a lighted cross with their decorations. I was very glad to see these reminders that the Christmas event can't be separated from the redeeming act the Child of Bethlehem came to do on our behalf. The manger and the cross are bound together as one act of God's gracious love for mankind. All of the lights and decorations are festive as they should be for the celebration of this birth. But it is the cross that brought us our greatest gift, life in Jesus Christ our Lord.

Christmas Day

For to us a child is born, to us a son is given,
and the government will be on his shoulders.
And he will be called Wonderful Counselor, Mighty God,
Everlasting Father, Prince of Peace.
Of the greatness of his government and peace there will be no end.
He will reign on David's throne and over his kingdom,
establishing and upholding it with justice and righteousness
from that time on and forever.
The zeal of the LORD Almighty will accomplish this.
(Isaiah 9:6-8)

"Do not be afraid;
for behold, I bring you good news of great joy
which will be for all the people;
for today in the city of David there has been born for you a Savior,
who is Christ the Lord."
(Luke 2:10-11)

We have no greater gift. It is ours free and without cost.
May the joy and strength of the risen and living Christ
be with you this Christmas Day and always.
The Stapfs

YESTERDAY'S TRUTH FOR ALL YEAR LONG

Today is more than a day for taking out the trash from all the gift wrapping paper and sorting out the presents to keep and those to be returned. It is more than searching for after Christmas bargains and merchants getting ready for the next holiday sale. Tradition in many areas notes today as the first of the twelve days of Christmas leading up to Epiphany and the coming of the Wise Men on January sixth. Even apart from tradition Christmas can't be dismissed easily. God has come among us. In a wonderful and mysterious way He has bound Himself to His creation, and promised to complete the purpose for which we were made. Jesus is not only the reason for this season, He is the reason for life itself. The Baby of Bethlehem came to redeem us from the power of sin and death, giving life to all who come to Him. That is not a decoration to be put away until next year. It is the joy in which we live and the reason for our humble worship every day.

Growing Deeper Each Day

Some people talk about the "after Christmas blues". Everything builds up to the celebration of the day, and then it is over. But it isn't really over. The writer of Hebrews tells us that "Jesus Christ is the same yesterday, today, and forever". (Hebrews 13:8) All of the decorations, gifts, and gatherings were fun, but they quickly pass into memories, and a few digital pictures. It is like that new car we wanted, or some fancy gadget. Once we have it the appeal wears off, and soon needs to be replaced by something newer. This is not so with the gift we received in the manger. Life in Jesus Christ should and can grow deeper with every new day of grace. God's grace in Jesus Christ is a treasure that can never be exhausted, can never grow old. So, we may feel some let down after the Christmas celebration, but always be reminded that "the reason for the season" will never let you down.

CHRISTMAS IS NEVER OVER

Christmas is over. The packages have been opened. Merchants are having their sales, and already planning for the next season. Such is the pace of our world, but is Christmas really over? Can it ever be? We celebrated the birth of God's only begotten Son, the second person of the Holy Trinity, entering our world, living our life, coming with the single purpose of making atonement for the sins of all mankind. That can never be over. We will gather for worship this coming Sunday to hear His word, to confess our faith in Him, and to receive His real presence in the holy sacrament. He is still alive and active in our world and in our life by the power of the Holy Spirit. The world will go on with all of its activities, but the reality of Christmas is never over. And that doesn't mean just some general feeling of peace and good will toward men. It means we celebrate Immanuel, God with us, now and always.

BUT AS FOR ME....

Most of Psalm 52 speaks of the evil people do and their rejection of the good God desires. Then it ends with these last two verses. "But as for me, I am like a green olive tree in the house of God; I trust in the lovingkindness of God forever and ever. I will give You thanks forever, because You have done it, And I will wait on Your name, for it is good, in the presence of Your godly ones." (Psalm 52: 8-9) A few words often catches my attention. "But as for me..." I don't know what you have before you this day. We all have our trials, and schedules, and demands. We all live in this broken world with it many uncertainties and fears. "But as for me ... I trust in the lovingkindness of God forever and ever." Lovingkindness is what we see when we look in the manger. The manger which we know is overshadowed by the cross. That is the lovingkindness of our God in giving us life and strength. Whatever it is that we must deal with today, we make our response "but as for me. "

Peace In The Midst Of Confusion

We live in a chaotic world with many uncertainties. We have our own pressures of schedules, deadlines, physical needs and so forth. Into the midst of this Jesus has told us repeatedly not to worry or be anxious. But how could we not? There are so many needs, so many things we can't control. The Old Testament prophet Isaiah had written "You will keep in perfect peace those whose minds are steadfast, because they trust in you. Trust in the LORD forever, for the LORD, the LORD himself, is the Rock eternal."(Isaiah 26:3&4) There is a rock, a solid place, in the midst of life, all life, especially the stressful life in which we live. Behind all of the many things we have to do is the sure and certain knowledge that our Lord is there. His strength is sufficient for this day, and this need. We remind ourselves of that rock many times during our day. He is our strength and our life in the midst of this world.

SUDDENLY

A man and his wife were vacation in Indonesia. He was standing on the beach taking photos of a volcanic island off shore. Suddenly he saw a wall of water rolling in across the bay. He had to turn and flee inland to save his life. Things can happen in just that manner. Some shepherds were sitting around the evenings campfire guarding their flock on a normal day like hundreds of other days before it. Suddenly an angel of the Lord appeared to them announcing the birth a baby, a very special baby, in the nearby village of Bethlehem. The lives of the mother and father of that baby had been turned completely around by the announcement of that unexpected birth. And that child, the Lord Jesus Christ, when grown, promised that He would be coming again suddenly and unexpectedly to complete God's plan for mankind. How does one prepare for such sudden and unexpected events? I don't know that there is a particular preparation for a tsunami, but a life lived in a humble and trusting relationship with the Lord is the daily preparation to which we are all called.